MacArthur's Navy

THE
SEVENTH FLEET
AND THE
BATTLE FOR
THE PHILIPPINES

MACARTHUR'S NAVY

EDWIN P. HOYT

 ORION BOOKS / NEW YORK

Published by Orion Books, a division of Crown Publishers, Inc., 201 East 50th Street, New York, New York 10022

ORION and colophon are trademarks of Crown Publishers, Inc.

Printed in the U.S.A.

Library of Congress Cataloging-in-Publication Data

Hoyt, Edwin Palmer.
  MacArthur's navy / Edwin P. Hoyt.
    p. cm.
    1. United States. Navy. Fleet, 7th—History. 2. MacArthur, Douglas, 1880–1964. 3. World War, 1939–1945—Naval operations, American. 4. World War, 1939–1945—Campaigns—Pacific Area.
I. Title.
D773.H69 1989   89-3386
940.54'5973—dc20

ISBN 0-517-56769-5

Design by Jake Victor Thomas

10 9 8 7 6 5 4 3 2 1

First Edition

CONTENTS

CONTENTS

MacARTHUR'S NAVY

1

SAD BEGINNINGS

After the Japanese opened the Pacific War on December 7, 1941, with their lightning-like strike against Pearl Harbor, the tide of battle seemed to move irremediably their way.

At the end of the first week of the war, Hong Kong was under attack. The Imperial Japanese Army was marching down the Malay Peninsula toward Singapore. Guam was captured. Wake Island was under siege. Japanese tanks took over Shanghai. Borneo was invaded.

Then came two events more significant for the future than the string of defeats the Western powers had been suffering in the early weeks of 1942: Admiral Thomas C. Hart moved the Asiatic Fleet down to the Dutch East Indies to fight under Field Marshal Archibald Wavell, and soon General Douglas MacArthur moved out of the Bataan Peninsula, where he had gone to direct the forlorn American defense of the Philippines. Thus were put into motion the forces that would create MacArthur's Navy.

The American Asiatic Fleet was not really a fleet in the normal sense of the word. Its flagship was a cruiser, it had no battleships, and the only vessel capable of carrying land-based aircraft was the old carrier *Langley*, which was no longer suitable for flight operations. The real assets of the Asiatic Fleet, and the only warships to survive, was the fleet of submarines. During the months of February and March 1942, the surface warships of the fleet tried their hardest, but one after another they were searched out and sunk by superior Japanese naval forces, superior and more modern. Finally the sea command of the area passed to the Dutch admiral E. E. Helfrich, and he superintended the Allied side of the battles that soon reduced the Allied Forces to a handful of scattered ships.

Thus by the spring of 1942 all that was left of the Asiatic Fleet were the submarines and some service ships, which were sent to Australia to continue the battle against Japan. Originally Admiral Hart had twenty-nine submarines, including six of the old S-boats (800 tons, 14 knots) and twenty-three "fleet submarines" (1,500 tons, 20 knots) of various classes. These were more than three hundred feet long, carried ten torpedo tubes and twenty-four torpedoes, a distinct improvement over the S class.

The Asiatic Fleet submarine force had moved out of the Philippines on December 31, 1941. Captain Wilkes, the commander, decided that day that he could no longer operate from Corregidor Island because of the constant Japanese bombing of the submarine base. The submarines were forced to submerge and stay down all day, and come up at night for maintenance and repair work. There were several hundred submarine specialists at the base, but only ten submarines left there at the time. Each could carry its own crew and ten passengers. So on that day, the submarines left the Philippines, carrying 250 extra men. Captain James Fife and half the Asiatic Fleet submarine force set off for Darwin to establish a base that was to serve General Douglas MacArthur, who was to command the new American war effort in the Southwest Pacific. Captain Wilkes went off to Surabaya to fight with the British and the Dutch. So thus, with half the force of the Asiatic Fleet, was born MacArthur's Navy.

One of the first actions of this new "navy" was that of the U.S.S. *Seawolf,* under Lieutenant Commander Frederick

B. Warder. She left Darwin on January 27, 1943, carrying thirty-seven tons of .50-caliber ammunition to the defenders of Corregidor. A week later the *Trout* sailed with 3,500 rounds of ammunition for the three-inch guns of Corregidor. The *Seadragon* went on patrol, sank the Japanese *Tamagawa Maru,* which was carrying troops and equipment south, and then went into Corregidor to take off the members of the naval radio intelligence unit, on orders from Admiral Ernest J. King, the chief of naval operations, who had decided that these people were too valuable to be captured by the enemy. On February 19 the *Swordfish* brought out Philippines Commonwealth President Manuel Quezon and his family and later U.S. High Commissioner Francis B. Sayre and his family. The U.S.S. *Sargo* also participated in such missions. Altogether in February, 1942, there were still twenty-six submarines of the Asiatic Fleet then operating, most of them from Australia. But after the cruiser *Houston* was sunk and the Battle of the Java Sea was lost to the Japanese, the end came for the fleet, and everything left was moved down to Australia. There was the Darwin base, under Captain Fife, and then the Fremantle base, near Perth, commanded by Captain Wilkes.

Until the last, the submarines from Australia tried to help out the defenders of Corregidor, bringing a small supply of ammunition and food and medicine. But it was inadequate, there was not enough help even to begin to tip the scales. The last contact with "the rock" was made at the end of April 1942, when Lieutenant Commander James Dempsey in the *Spearfish* took out the records of the men who would soon become prisoners of war, along with twenty-five officers and army nurses.

By summer, General MacArthur was beginning to plan his fight back. The immediate impetus of action was aimed at Japanese landings in southern New Guinea, which was Australian territory. The Japanese made successful landings at Lae and Salamaua and planned to occupy Port Moresby. From there they planned further to assault the

Australian sea lanes and air space, and ultimately to take over Samoa, the French New Hebrides Islands, and finally, Australia itself. MacArthur's first task, then, was to manage the defense of New Guinea and then move to the assault as soon as possible.

In the defense of New Guinea, the American navy was of little use. The war was primarily a jungle war, and there were no naval surface forces available in the Pacific to send to General MacArthur. He had to make do with what the Australians could muster.

The way that the navy could help just then was to continue to increase the submarine campaign out of Australia. In the summer of 1942 Captain Ralph Christie was sent from a European assignment to Brisbane with a number of the old S-boats. Captain Charles A. Lockwood was sent to Fremantle to replace Captain Wilkes and was soon promoted to Rear Admiral.

That summer of 1942 General MacArthur was fretting over the decision made by President Roosevelt that the war against Hitler was to take precedence over the war against Japan. He asked for a battle fleet, including two aircraft carriers, to help him prosecute the war in the Southwest Pacific. Instead of ships, Admiral King sent him a new admiral, Rear Admiral Arthur S. Carpender, who had the grand title of Commander of U.S. Naval Forces, Southwest Pacific, and no forces except the submarines, and virtually nothing to do. For the first month or two Carpender's major occupation was to try to persuade the submariners to take Australian mutton and rabbit on their patrols instead of demanding beef. The admiral very nearly created a mutiny in the submarine service.

At the end of July 1942, Admiral Lockwood had twenty submarines, operating out of Perth, and Captain Christie had the S-boat command, operating out of Brisbane. By this time the Brisbane force had become MacArthur's Navy, in the sense that he had a hand in the decisions as to where the patrols were to go.

MacArthur wanted them to go up around the Bismarcks, to scout Rabaul and Kavieng, two important Japanese base areas, and to keep track of what the enemy was up to. Thus the *S-44* was sent to Kavieng in July. She was patrolling off Kavieng at the northwest end of New Ireland Island on August 10, just three days after the Marines invaded Guadalcanal. Her commander, Lieutenant Commander J. R. Moore, saw several Japanese warships through his periscope. These were the cruisers and destroyers of Cruiser Division 6, which was just returning north from its overwhelming victory at Savo Island, where the cruisers had sunk four American cruisers without a single loss.

Skipper Moore torpedoed the last cruiser in the line as it came by and thus sank the Imperial Japanese Navy's ship *Kako*. The exploit gave MacArthur's Navy a "first." The *Kako* was the first major Japanese warship to be sunk by a submarine in the Pacific War.

The invasion of Guadalcanal was purely a navy show. Admiral King had insisted on it, although General MacArthur, and even King's own Admiral Robert Ghormley, said the Americans in the area did not have the resources to support such an invasion. They were right, but they were also wrong; in spite of the deficiencies, the Americans managed to hang on at Guadalcanal. One result of Guadalcanal was an effective split in the whole command of the entire area, much to the discomfiture of General MacArthur. Rear Admiral Robert Ghormley took over the new South Pacific command, and he did get some ships, but General MacArthur still did not. Instead, Admiral Carpender moved to Brisbane, with the implied promise that his new command of MacArthur's Navy would soon mean ships. But then Admiral King decided that all the squabbling about submarine operations in the southern part of the Pacific had to be stopped, so he put Captain Christie and the Brisbane submarine force under the direct command of Admiral Halsey, thus depriving Admiral Carpender and General MacArthur of their naval force. MacArthur complained to the Joint Chiefs of Staff, but all he got out of it was the assignment of six submarines for his purposes. The battle between the general and Washington was not going very well for MacArthur. At the time it was not regarded as very important by the Joint Chiefs, because the big naval action was off Guadalcanal, and the New Guinea show was basically a land and air struggle.

At the end of 1942 came more disappointment for the general and the Southwest Pacific command. Admiral King ordered most of the submarines to move back to Pearl Harbor for operational control. Captain Christie was ordered to Washington to see what could be done about the defective American submarine torpedoes (which often did not explode at all), and Captain Fife was made commander of what was left of MacArthur's Navy, one squadron of submarines and the tender *Fulton*, at Brisbane. Then came more musical chairs: Admiral Lockwood succeeded to command of the Pacific Fleet submarine force at Pearl Harbor, and Captain Christie was made an admiral and sent back to Australia. General MacArthur now became louder in his demand for a navy. He intended to move up the north coast of New Guinea, he said, and he absolutely had to have naval support ships to do so. So the Joint Chiefs of Staff took that matter under advisement at the end of 1942.

In the beginning of 1943, General MacArthur was in a position to do something for the first time to help the men left behind in the Philippines. The Corregidor force had surrendered in May 1942, but several hundred American soldiers had escaped at one time or another into the southern Philippines and, with members of the Philippine Constabulary and others, had formed guerrilla organizations on several of the islands. These were harrying the Japanese and causing a certain amount of trouble useful to MacArthur.

In January 1943, MacArthur sent the submarine *Gudgeon* to Negros Island with Filipino Major Jesus Villamor and six tons of medical supplies and weapons. Then he sent an American named Charles Parsons, a wartime naval lieutenant commander, who had long been resident in the Philippines, to analyze and organize the guerrillas. From this point on the submarines made regular missions to the Philippines to help the guerrillas. Other MacArthur submarines were evacuating crashed fliers from lonely islands and taking agents in and out to observe the activities of the Japanese enemy.

In March 1943, Admiral King set up a whole new naval organization in the Southwest Pacific to placate General MacArthur. The navy established the Seventh Fleet and promoted Carpender to Vice-Admiral. Still, however, MacArthur's Navy was almost entirely an underseas navy and would continue to be during that spring and summer. The big change would come when General MacArthur was really in a position to take the initiative and would need naval forces to move his troops and to support them in their landings.

2

CHANGE OF COMMAND

By January 1, 1943, the war situation in the southern Pacific area had changed drastically. The Japanese had occupied the northeast coast of New Guinea in March 1942, and had maintained naval superiority for months. With that and with air superiority as well, they had landed troops at Buna toward the end of July. In August they had launched an overland attack along the Kokoda trail, which runs to Port Moresby, but were defeated by Australian and American troops there and at Milne Bay, on the eastern tip of the island.

Then the Australian Seventh Division and the American Thirty-second Infantry Division had again defeated the Japanese at Buna and Gona on the east coast, and by the beginning of January the Japanese were evacuating this part of New Guinea, as well as preparing to move out of Guadalcanal. General MacArthur in New Guinea, and Admiral Halsey in the southern Solomons, had seized the initiative from the Japanese.

Early in January Rear Admiral Daniel E. Barbey had been brought to Australia to take command of the Seventh Fleet Amphibious Force. It would be his task to deliver General MacArthur's troops to areas that were to be invaded and then to protect them until the invasion was secure on the beaches.

For the first time MacArthur really had his navy now. It consisted of a small assortment of Australian and American ships, which formed a transport division. Generally speaking, major warships would have to be borrowed from Admiral C. W. Nimitz's Pacific Fleet, because there were not enough ships yet in the Pacific to go around for all the operations in the planning stages.

During the winter months of 1943, the troops of the newly created Sixth Army first recuperated from their intensive fighting in Buna and Gona, and then began to train for amphibious operations. Meanwhile Admiral Barbey tried to put together an invasion force of sorts.

He secured a repair ship, and although it did not have the communications facilities needed, he made this his flagship. Her name was the U.S.S. *Regal*. He secured assignment of some landing ships designed to carry tanks (LSTs), and he arranged to borrow some more from Admiral Halsey's South Pacific command for amphibious operations.

General MacArthur's headquarters was planning operations to isolate Rabaul, the big Japanese military base on New Britain Island, which was the center of Japanese operations for the Southern Pacific area. The plan was called Elkton. It involved combined operations by General MacArthur's and by Admiral Halsey's forces.

First would come the capture of Woodlark and Kiriwina islands and then the seizure of airfields on the Huon Peninsula of eastern New Guinea. This would be accomplished by MacArthur's troops.

Second would be the capture of the New Georgia Group in the southern Solomons. This would be done by Admiral Halsey's forces.

Third would come an assault on Bougainville Island, also by Halsey.

Fourth would be the capture of Kavieng.

As it worked out, first came the capture of the undefended Russell Islands off the tip of Guadalcanal by

Admiral Halsey on February 21, 1943. Next came the capture of the New Georgia group that summer.

And, simultaneous with the New Georgia operation, General MacArthur's Navy was to go into action as a striking force for the first time. Admiral Barbey would deliver the troops to capture Woodlark and Kiriwina islands, which were supposed to be valuable for air bases.

Woodlark and Kiriwina islands lie in the Solomon Sea, both off the southeast coast of New Guinea. Kiriwina is about a hundred and twenty-five miles south of New Britain Island (Rabaul); Woodlark is more than two hundred miles southwest of Bougainville Island. Together they would give the Allies powerful bases for staging air strikes against Rabaul, or so it was then believed.

When scouts and survey groups were sent to these islands to check on them, they discovered that the islands had never been occupied by the Japanese. This certainly made Admiral Barbey's task much simpler. But there were still plenty of problems. Kiriwina, for example, did not have a single "good" beach on its twenty-five mile length. Woodlark, forty-four miles long, had beaches that ran only a few hundred yards and then smacked into coral cliffs. And on Woodlark what was not coral was thick jungle.

The U.S. Joint Chiefs of Staff—the heads of all the armed services—had decided in Washington that the most important reason for capturing these islands was to give Admiral Barbey's amphibious forces practice.

After several changes in timing, finally on June 21, Admiral Barbey's ships left Australia for Woodlark Island, carrying the men of the 20th Naval Construction Battalion and men of the 112th Cavalry Regiment, who would protect them ashore. Another group of ships carried the force that would land on Kiriwina. The Kiriwina force consisted of the 158th U.S. Army Regimental Combat Team and the 46th Engineer Combat Company.

The landings on Woodlark were accomplished on June 22, without any opposition at all since there were no Japanese there, and the landings on Kiriwina were similar on June 23. After that first group of engineers landed on Kiriwina, they got together some native help and built a coral causeway 300 yards long.

The landings were difficult, and made more so by the coral reefs. But not a ship was lost, nor a landing craft, nor a man. So the landings were successful in spite of nervousness and clumsiness on this first attempt.

The engineers then began to build the airfields. Woodlark was hardly even bombed by the Japanese; one day a single Japanese plane came over and dropped five small bombs. That was all. But Kiriwina was bombed several times during the construction of the airfields that summer. By midsummer a Fifth Air Force fighter squadron was moved to Kiriwina. But Woodlark was never used as an operational air base. In fact, the war moved so fast that summer of 1943 that it was not long before both islands were virtually forgotten as necessary for the purpose of isolating Rabaul.

In the fall of 1943 General MacArthur began to move along the northern shore of New Guinea. His purpose was to secure a jumping-off point for the invasion of the Philippines. The navy at this time was successfully conducting its Central Pacific campaign, driving to the Gilberts, and later on would drive to the Marshall Islands. The Central Pacific drive was then planned to move to Saipan, inside the Inner Empire of Japan, and then to end in a move to the China coast or to Japan itself. But MacArthur was steadfast in his own view, which was that the return to the Philippines was vital, for political as well as for military reasons. So General MacArthur continued his operations and his planning to that end.

So it was that in November 1943 the men of the Australian Ninth Division marched along the Huon Peninsula, driving the Japanese garrison out of Finschhafen. During this period Admiral Barbey's amphibious force was given the painful but necessary task of moving supplies and troops up the coast, because the roads were impossible and the airfields were not yet completed. So it was mid-November before the ships and sailors could be released to undertake the next amphibious operation of MacArthur's Navy, the attack against Cape Gloucester, which guards the Vitiaz and Dampier straits.

Meanwhile, all that spring, summer, and fall, the offensive of MacArthur's Navy against the Japanese had been carried by the submarines. They grew ever more active in the South and Southwest Pacific areas, and the Japanese responded with a new antisubmarine campaign that sent Japanese "hunter-killer" teams into the waters around the Solomons and the Philippines. One such team apparently accounted for the end of the submarine *Triton,* which went out from Captain Fife's Brisbane command in February 1943, bound for the Rabaul area. The *Triton* was not heard from after Captain Fife warned that three destroyers were coming into its patrol area. All that did come in was a report from the *Trigger,* operating nearby, about a Japanese attack on another submarine.

By spring the submarines from Australia were also operating off the Strait of Malacca, around the Malay Peninsula and Sumatra. The water was very shallow and Admiral Christie objected to sending in submarines, but they were needed to prevent Japanese supplies from reaching the Rangoon area. The *Grenadier* fell victim to the shallow water. One day in April her captain spotted a convoy but was forced down by Japanese planes. The captain dived her down to 130 feet, but that was not enough and that day she was depth-bombed and wrecked by Japanese bombs. The American crew was captured, taken to Penang, interrogated, tortured, and then sent to a prison camp in Japan. Nearly all of them survived the war.

By the summer of 1943 the submarines from Australia were making "milk runs" to the Philippines, bringing guerrilla leaders back and forth, carrying in supplies, and taking out intelligence about Japanese activity. The *Grayling* was one of these. She took supplies to Panay Island in July and then went to the Manila area to patrol. But there, in Lingayen Gulf, she was lost. And the *Cisco* was also lost in the fall of 1943, due largely to inadequate maintenance, because the submarine commands were so widely separated and supplies were so scarce. She went out with a faulty hydraulic system, leaving Fremantle and stopping off at Darwin to refuel. She never came back.

By November all the plans were made for the seizure of Cape Gloucester, which then was regarded as very important, since the cape lies at the far end of New Britain Island from Rabaul, the Japanese center of activity. If the Americans could take Cape Gloucester, they could march overland to attack Rabaul, while it was also attacked from the air and from the sea.

To undertake the land attack, General MacArthur had Lieutenant General Walter Krueger's Sixth Army. At sea, MacArthur had the Seventh Fleet.

That summer and fall of 1943 General MacArthur's forces were preparing for large-scale strategic operations in the future. The First Marine Division had been brought out of Guadalcanal after the conquest of the Japanese on that island, and had been taken down to the Melbourne area to get rid of their malaria and to rest up after their heroic conflict. At first about seventy-five hundred men were down with malaria and other tropical diseases, but the temperate climate of Melbourne and the availability of medicines soon cut that number to the bone. The men of the division relaxed and regained their strength. Then they began training again. They got the new M-1 Garand rifle to replace the old Springfield 1903 models that had been standard American infantry weapons for forty years.

In April and May 1943, the Fifth Marines practiced assault landings on the beaches of Port Phillip Bay, near Melbourne. They had the use of the only attack transport in MacArthur's Navy, the U.S.S. *Henry T. Allen,* which had been sent over by Admiral Halsey from Nouméa. They began to get to know the LST and the LCI (landing craft infantry).

The Seventeenth Marines soon moved up to Goodenough Island, which would be the base for the Marines until they were assigned to an amphibious operation. Soon the other two elements of the division, the Fifth Marines and Seventh Marines, joined the Seventeenth. So combat training began again at Oro Bay in New Guinea.

From the beginning Admiral Barbey had to make do with very little equipment in his training of this Southwest Pacific assault force. The landing exercises were held at Taupota Bay on the north shore of New Guinea. In the beginning the performance was miserable. On the first landing attempt on October 22, one LST took three hours to unload, and another took four and a half hours. At that rate, Admiral Barbey observed, they were not going to get anywhere.

But the men kept at it. There were more landings on October 27 and October 28, and the techniques improved fast. The unloading time for an LST was cut to less than an hour, and by mid-November the navy men were old hands and the landings seemed easy.

The new equipment came in. The LVT, or amphibious tractor, was the best of all. It could carry 4,500 pounds of cargo in to the beach. And a later model could carry 6,500 pounds. Once it reached the beach, this "alligator" could smash through the jungle and thus make a rude road for other vehicles.

Early in December 1943, the troops began to move up to Cape Sudest, the point at which they would load for landing on New Britain Island and the assault on the Japanese stronghold. The plan called for them to land in the Borgen Bay-Tauali area and then establish beachheads. They were to capture the Cape Gloucester airfields and to secure western New Britain to the Itni River line.

So Admiral Barbey got ready for the new operation. He had nine destroyer transports, twenty-three LSTs, nineteen LCIs, twelve LCTs (landing craft tank), and fourteen LCMs (landing craft medium). For the protection of this landing force he had two destroyers and two rocket-equipped amphibious trucks called DUKWs, or "ducks," plus another twelve destroyers and two rocket-firing LCIs to cover the landings on the eastern side of Cape Gloucester. And to support all, there was British Rear Admiral V. A. C. Crutchley's force of two Australian cruisers, two American cruisers, and eight destroyers. So much had MacArthur's Navy grown by December 1943, on the eve of the Cape Gloucester landings.

3

LANDINGS ON NEW BRITAIN

A dmiral Barbey had a serious problem with the geography of New Britain Island, the site of Japan's most powerful base in all the South Pacific. Dampier Strait, which connects the Bismarck Sea and the Solomon Sea, is narrow and so full of reefs, and in 1943 was so little known to American hydrographers, that the admiral did not want to commit his capital ships to the dangerous waters. So when it came time to plan for a landing on Cape Gloucester on New Britain, he chose a route that was longer but safer, around Rooke Island and Tolokiwa Island.

The prize for the Allies was a pair of airstrips, one completed and one not, on the grassland near Dorf Point, between Mount Talawe and Mount Tangi.

The area was defended by the Japanese Seventeenth Infantry Division, whose troops had been brought to New Britain by destroyer transport. By the end of 1943, aircraft of the Eleventh Air Fleet at Rabaul were warning that a landing was imminent. But one of the problems of the Allies was a paucity of information. Admiral Carpender, the commander of the Seventh Fleet, had already shown himself in the battle for Buna and Gona as so conservative that he would not risk ships. He refused to send even torpedo boats north of Cape Gloucester, and thus Admiral Barbey had very little knowledge of what the invasion fleet was going to find.

It was not until after Admiral Carpender was relieved of command of the Seventh Fleet by Vice-Admiral Thomas C. Kinkaid that a greater effort began. During the second week of December PT boats did penetrate the area and land scouts, who made contact with some of the sixteen coast watchers and gained information about what the landing troops would encounter. They discovered, among other things, that there might be as many as twelve hundred enemy troops in the area of the island to be attacked.

The first landing was to be made on a peninsula lying off Cape Merkus. Three islands lie off the shore, the isles of Arawe, Ausak, and Pilelo. The beach—Beach Orange—was inshore from these islands. The reason for choosing this point for the landings was that by landing at Arawe, the Allies could put an end to the Japanese barge traffic that took supplies along the coast. That sort of travel, by boat, was the only practical way for the Japanese to supply several garrisons that were cut off from each other by jungle and swamp. The American landings were to be led by Brigadier General Julian W. Cunningham, commander of the U.S. 112th Cavalry Regiment.

The arrangements for these landings indicate just how short of vessels and supplies the Seventh Fleet was and how difficult the operations of Admiral Barbey's amphibious command were going to be.

Admiral Barbey was enormously short of ships. A handful of LSTs so valuable that he hesitated to risk them in these shallow waters, a landing ship dock called the *Carter Hall,* and the Australian transport *Westralia* were about all that he could find. He also had several destroyer transports, those overage destroyers that were still doing valuable service in the Pacific although their days as first-class fighting ships were long past. It was decided that the LSTs would not be used at Arawe, and after the initial landings—which would be carried out by troops in the destroyer transports, going in to shore in rubber boats—the main force would land in LVTs, or landing vehicle tanks, LCVPs, and LCMS, more landing craft. The landing craft would be manned by Marines of the First Marine Division and by engineers of the Second Engineer Special Brigade.

As D-Day approached, Admiral Barbey worried. No one really knew anything about the reef around that part of the island. So he ordered the use of LVTs (amphibious tractors) to carry the first waves in, and Brigadier Cunningham got twenty-nine LVTs for the job. They also got nine new Buffalo Amphtracs on loan. These were manned by Marines of the First Amphibious Tractor Battalion.

Protection for the Arawe force was a problem, because of the shallow water. Lieutenant Commander Morton C. Mumma, of the PT boat force, assigned two boats from the base at Dreger Harbor on New Guinea to patrol each night. Another two PT boats were assigned to patrol for Japanese barges that might be bringing reinforcements. And two more would scout around Kiriwina to be sure no reinforcements came from that direction.

On December 5, 1943, the *Carter Hall* loaded up with marine tractors and crewmen, and the *Westralia* picked up its troops. The two destroyer transports *Sands* and *Humphreys* and the assault troops came to shore to practice landings. They would have only one practice landing as it turned out, because time was short.

The practice landing was not very satisfactory. The young officers showed that they did not have enough training, and some of the troops went astray. But there was nothing to be done except to go over the mistakes; there was no time to hold another landing because D-Day was December 15.

No one was quite sure how many Japanese the Americans would encounter in the Arawe area. Originally the intelligence estimate indicated that there were probably only about one hundred fifty defenders, but a few days before the landings were scheduled, pilots of observation planes spotted a number of barges moving in that area, and so the estimate had to be raised to about five hundred defenders.

On December 13 the landing force loaded at Good-enough. General MacArthur came down to watch the LVTs and the two rocket-firing DUKWs load on the *Carter Hall* and the *Westralia*. The usual ship's boats on the latter were replaced by sixteen LCVPs and two LCMs. The men of the attack force also loaded aboard the two destroyers, *Humphreys* and *Sands*.

At midnight the convoy sailed for Buna, and there General Cunningham joined them, boarding the destroyer *Conyngham*, which was Admiral Barbey's command ship. Indeed this was a shoestring operation, for nowhere else in the Pacific campaign was a commanding admiral riding in a destroyer!

On December 14 the task force headed for its destination across the Solomon Sea, escorted by Admiral Crutchley's cruiser force. Nine destroyers escorted the transports.

The convoy had been sighted by the Japanese even before it set out. A float plane had flown over the loading area and dropped a bomb. More important, the pilot had reported back to his base, and in Rabaul, Admiral Kusaka had been alerted. There were, said the report, five transports and five destroyers moving somewhere in the area. He ordered the Eleventh Air Fleet to launch an attack at dawn.

The convoy reached the unloading area, and by four o'clock in the morning operations began. By 5 A.M. the two big ships had unloaded their troops and equipment and had started back for New Guinea.

The first group of soldiers paddled in across the shallow water in rubber boats. The two destroyers carrying troops stood offshore, unloaded the men into landing craft, and then withdrew because the shallow water was too dangerous for them.

The intelligence officers had wondered if the landings would really be opposed. At 5:22 they got the answer.

Automatic weapons opened up on the men in the fifteen rubber boats and in a few minutes sank all but three of them. The destroyer *Shaw* then opened fire on the beach and sent off several salvos of five-inch shells. The Japanese stopped firing. Gradually the landings proceeded, covered by gunfire from the ships offshore, and by midafternoon the American beachhead was well established.

They discovered that there were actually only 120 Japanese defending this islet, and most of them had escaped to the main island of New Britain. So the Japanese defense was still to be heard from.

In the air it was a different story. Admiral Kusaka had given the order for attack by the Eleventh Air Fleet. The Americans had expected a strong air attack, so a squadron of P-38 fighter planes had been sent to cover the landings. That morning at around 8 A.M. a squadron of enemy fighters attacked and engaged the P-38s. Then, about forty Japanese fighters and bombers hit the beachhead. All the ships but the *Conyngham* had already left the landing area, so there was very little antiaircraft support for the beachhead. The landing craft bearing equipment had just moved in to the beachhead when the Japanese struck. The Japanese blew up one LCVP. But the guns on shore, 50-caliber machine guns and 20-mm cannon, were enough to keep the Japanese careful. After a little while, more American fighters appeared, and the danger seemed to be over.

The landings were secure. For the next week the Japanese continued to launch air attacks on the island area, but American planes usually arrived to drive them off. During this period, however, one escort coastal transport was sunk, and a minesweeper and seven LCTs were badly damaged. But by the beginning of the fourth week of December the Japanese air attacks on the area had dwindled. General Cunningham moved his command post ashore and began sending out patrols to discover the disposition of the Japanese in West New Britain, before the landings of the main force in what was called Operation Backhander.

21

There were lots of Japanese about, moving around the area in motor-driven barges, which were the best craft for the shallow water. Major Shinjiro Komori, the commander of the Japanese garrison, made several attacks on the airfield area, but the Americans drove them all off.

All this, of course, was in preparation for the main landings at Cape Gloucester.

On December 20 and 21, the troops rehearsed at Cape Sudest, and for once the rehearsal went very smoothly. The amphibious training program was finally working. So Admiral Barbey prepared once more to move out with Task Force Seventy-six, in the flagship *Conyngham*. Admiral Kinkaid, with the Allied naval forces of the Seventh Fleet, would cover these landings and the Fifth Army Air Force would fly air support.

In the past few weeks the forces assembled in this part of the Pacific had grown a good deal. How the war had turned around! In the early days of Guadalcanal, sixteen months earlier, the Japanese had clear air superiority over the Solomons and New Guinea, but now it was reversed. The planes of the Fifth Air Force, based in Australia and New Guinea, bombed and strafed the Japanese installations on New Britain every day in preparation for the landings. Between December 1 and D-Day the bombers dropped 3,200 tons of bombs in the Cape Gloucester area, flying 1,500 sorties. The air support really knocked out the Japanese defenses before the troops arrived, and the troops of the Japanese defending force, commanded by Major General Iwao Matsuda, who was entrusted with the defense of West New Britain, hid in the jungles. Meanwhile Admiral Barbey's amphibious forces got ready for the coming landings, and on Christmas Eve, 1943, they were ready to go.

4

CAPE GLOUCESTER

I n the darkness of the small hours of Christmas morning, 1943, Admiral Barbey's amphibious force sailed out from Cape Sudest on New Guinea, bound for the landing zone on New Britain Island. It was hot and muggy, and they were heading into rain. What they might expect from the Japanese no one quite knew, for although the war was going against Japan with more and more certainty, the enemy still had a large capability, if he wanted to exert it.

The convoy consisted of LSTs and other landing ships and nine destroyer transports. The *Conyngham* led them out, with Admiral Barbey aboard. This time the troop commander, also on board the flagship, was Marine Major General William H. Rupertus of the First Marine Division. The Marines would make this important landing for General MacArthur, who now was confident that he was on his way back to the Philippines. The capture of Cape Gloucester would put finishing touches on the isolation of Rabaul, which was essential to that move, for once the one hundred thousand troops in Rabaul were taken effectively out of the war, the movement up New Guinea would become much easier, and from New Guinea the next step would be to the southern Philippines.

The ships moved through Vitiaz Strait, divided into Eastern and Western assault groups.

The purpose of the invasion was to capture the Cape Gloucester airfields and hold them. The landings were made quite easily; not even the Japanese naval air force made an appearance that day, and no Japanese were found until near dusk when a small group was located near the village of Sumeru. They moved into the jungle as soon as the Marines opened fire.

There was a reason for the lack of opposition. A Japanese coast watcher in the hills of New Guinea had spotted the Eastern assault group on its way and had reported it. But the coast watcher gave the indication that the landing force was heading for Cape Merkus, and so the Japanese defense effort was turned to a place where there would be no landings. Thus when Admiral Barbey's ships came in, they were unopposed.

The ships bound for the Yellow Beaches of Gloucester came through Vitiaz Strait in the dead of night and steamed along at twelve knots, protected by Admiral Crutchley's cruiser force. They were off the Cape Gloucester beaches by early morning and at 6 A.M. the cruiser force was delivering a bombardment of the shore.

This, too, was unopposed, as were the air strikes that began at dawn. Five squadrons of B-24 heavy bombers dropped 500-pound bombs on the beach area. A squadron of B-25 medium bombers dropped eight tons of white phosphorus smoke on Target Hill. This turned out to be a mistake, because soon the whole beach was so obscured that the shoreline approach lanes were hidden by H-hour, or landing time.

But, fortunately, the Japanese were simply not in evidence, so the landings proceeded with very few casualties, usually caused by a man stepping in a shell hole or hurt by a falling tree that had been weakened by the barrage.

The Japanese came into evidence a little later in the morning, when a small unit began firing to the west of the landings. At ten o'clock the Japanese let a column go through their lines and then opened up. Consequently Company K of the Seventh Marines lost its commander and its executive officer in a few minutes, both killed in action. The Marines had run into a system of bunkers that was very effectively placed. It took several hours to clear out the Japanese, and the Marines suffered a number of casualties in the task. But by the end of the morning the second echelon of supply ships was coming in to unload.

The arrival of the Japanese air force just about then precipitated a drama of tragic errors. The Japanese fighters came in and dove down on the ships offshore. At the same time a flight of B-25 bombers came low over the armada, and two of the B-25s were shot down by American gunners. Then the B-25s remaining moved over Silimati Point, and bombed and strafed the American positions there, thinking they were Japanese. One officer was killed, and so were fourteen enlisted men.

If there had not been much opposition in the beginning, the Japanese air force made up for it that afternoon. Nearly ninety planes came in to attack, and they concentrated their efforts on the ships offshore. As the Japanese arrived, so did two squadrons of P-38 fighter planes to protect the Allied ships. Soon the sky was full of dogfights. But the Japanese bombers waited, and attacked. The destroyer *Shaw* was crippled by bombs. The *Brownson* took two bombs behind the smokestack and sank in a few minutes, taking down 8 officers and 100 men. The battle ended, and the Americans counted fifty-seven Japanese planes shot down (later figures indicated the number was actually about twenty planes).

So the Japanese went home that day and they did not come back, largely because starting on December 27, the Fifth Air Force began sending so many planes to attack Rabaul that the Japanese defenders of the Eleventh Air Fleet were busy right at home all day long.

By evening of D-Day, the American beachhead on Cape Gloucester was secure. Eleven thousand men were ashore, and all the guns and vehicles that had been sent had been landed.

Now the battles were fought on land. The Japanese had about fourteen hundred men defending the airfields, and they rushed up reinforcements of seventeen hundred more men. The fighting became intense on the night of D-Day, and it lasted three days and three nights. The Marines captured Hell's Point after a hard struggle, and that paved the way for the taking of the airfields. The Marines moved forward on December 29, and captured Airfield No. 2. Two days later, after they also had Airfield No. 1, General Rupertus raised the American flag over Cape Gloucester to mark the capture and radioed General Krueger, commander of the Sixth Army, that the First Marine Division had done its job.

Having responded slowly, the Japanese in West New Britain then began to mount a number of serious counterattacks, trying to stem the Allied tide. Three of these attacks had been met and overcome by January 3 at Target Hill, the key to the Cape Gloucester defenses. All this while the men of MacArthur's Navy were doing a remarkable job of reinforcing the troops and supplying them, with scarcely any vessel larger than an LST. The real shortage of shipping and warships for the Southwest Pacific was always felt and nowhere more than in this New Britain operation.

The Marines fought through the *kunai* grass and the jungle to drive away the Japanese troops threatening the beachhead. Here is the official Marine account of one battle:

> The Fifth Company of the Second Battalion of the Imperial Japanese 141st Infantry Regiment was to make the attack on the Marines.
>
> The 5th Company of 2/141, supported by the direct fire of 20 mm cannon and machine guns firing from

positions in the jungle at the base of the hill and 75 mm guns emplaced near Hill 660, was to seize the crest of the hill.

The unit defending, the 3rd Platoon of Company A of the 1st Battalion of the 7th Marines, was ready when the assault came. Long before the Japanese actually started up the lower slopes, the marines on the narrow nose of the hill above the point of attack could hear enemy soldiers cutting steps into the steep base of the hill which was hidden in the jungle growth. The 1st Battalion's mortars, in position [in] back of the height, could not bear on the Japanese as they were actually as close as 20 yards to the Marines above them. The Japanese mortars and grenade launchers were not hampered by the same limitation and enemy shells landed all over the hill during the night to cover the attack preparations.

Toward dawn, the enemy soldiers rose out of the trenches they had dug to protect themselves from Marine fire and attempted to storm a machine gun position on the naked nose of ground. Although a Japanese mortar shell killed two men at the gun, the sole survivor of the crew stayed on and kept firing, cutting down the Japanese as they climbed into his line of sight. The rest of the Marine platoon, with the support of men from the various observation posts located on the hill's crest, used small arms and grenades to beat back every attempt of the enemy to gain the hill's upper slopes. By daylight although the Japanese were still firing on the hill, the counterattack proper had petered out. When it was safe to move about in the open later on during the morning of the third of January, patrols were sent out to probe the area from where the attack was launched. Forty bodies were found, many of them piled in heaps in the trenches at the hill's foot; the absence of any wounded was evidence that the cost of the fruitless attack must have been even greater. The Japanese themselves counted the casualties at Target Hill as 46 killed, 54 wounded and two missing in action.

The prize of the night's action was the documents taken from the body of the Japanese company commander who fell attacking the Marine machine-gun position. The papers helped the Intelligence Section fill in the gaps in the order of battle and gave them a pretty clear picture of the movement of the troops opposing them. A fragmentary order signed by this officer, and picked up from the body of one of his platoon leaders on January 4 gave the marines their first inkling of the existence of Aogiri Ridge, a formidable defensive position that guarded the trail over which most of the Japanese were reaching the battle area.

The Marines kept moving. They fought at Suicide Creek, and they fought on Aogiri Ridge, against the 1,350 Japanese remaining as the defensive line. It was slow, slogging work. On January 6, they moved ahead again, starting at 11 A.M., after a fifteen-minute barrage fired on Hill 150. Company A waded across a stream at the foot of Target Hill and advanced until it was stopped by the crackle of small-arms fire. They had hit a roadblock on the coastal trail. So tanks were brought up, and they were led across the stream by a half-track. Then up came the Sherman tanks, and their 75-mm guns knocked out the roadblock in short order. But of course there was another one, and another, and another. And they fought not only the Japanese but the monsoon, whose heavy rains had practically wiped out the trails.

After the Aogiri Ridge battle the First Marines counted the losses: 170 men killed since D-Day, 6 dead of wounds, and 4 of other causes, and 636 wounded. The Japanese had lost 2,400 killed and about the same number wounded, and the Americans had taken 11 prisoners of war.

The Marines went on. The next battles were fought at Hill 660, where the Japanese staged a whole series of banzai attacks. After three days of action on that hill, the Japanese had lost 200 dead and an equal number wounded, to the Marines' 50 killed and wounded.

The capture of Hill 660 marked the end of the land fighting for the Cape Gloucester area. By January 16, the Japanese had dug in around the Lupin airfield (which the Americans did not want), and eventually the Japanese discovered this in time to evacuate the remnants of General Komori's defense force. By the end of the month, General Krueger could report that the western part of New Britain was now securely in American hands. The Americans were building up the airfields on the cape, when suddenly they realized that the war was proceeding once more so rapidly that the airfields were really of very little value. But the work continued, and on January 28 the first planes landed on Airfield No. 2. The Thirty-fifth Fighter Squadron moved up to this field in February, and the Eightieth Squadron came a little later. But almost immediately they were withdrawn, to support General MacArthur's fast-moving drive along the New Guinea coast toward the Philippines. So the Cape Gloucester battles, although bloody and hard-fought all the way, really turned out to be a waste of time. By the end of February the Marines had cleared all the Japanese from the whole western area of New Britain, and nobody really cared. Admiral Barbey and the whole of MacArthur's Navy were occupied elsewhere by this time.

5

VICTORY IN
THE SOUTH PACIFIC

The Allies were moving up the coast of New Guinea and along the coast of New Britain. General Krueger planned a new assault on the Willaumez Peninsula to take the Japanese airfield at Hoskins. Meanwhile, an assault on the Admiralty Islands was demanding Admiral Barbey's major attention. On February 29 the navy landed troops of the First Cavalry Division on Negros Island, and the Admiralty's battle began. General MacArthur and Admiral Kinkaid came to watch the show.

At about seven-thirty that morning three B-24 heavy bombers bombed Momote. Ten minutes later the cruisers and destroyers of the fleet began shelling the island. It was a blustery, rainy day, and the flying weather was terrible. Several B-25s also struck the landing area, with bombs and strafing attacks. Before 1:00 P.M. the whole force was ashore, and casualties were only five men killed or wounded.

General MacArthur and Admiral Kinkaid went ashore later that afternoon. They learned that although they had first expected very light opposition, there were more Japanese on the island than they expected. So the decision had to be made—would this assault be regarded as a raid, and the troops withdrawn? General MacArthur decided not. The troops would remain and be reinforced. So two destroyers were called for to bring more troops, and two others were ordered to remain offshore to give fire support. They did so. By March 2, 1944, the troops had been reinforced, and the beachhead was secure.

Soon the troops had captured Manus Island as well, and with it they had gained control of Seeadler Harbor, one of the finest ship anchorages in the world, and one that would prove enormously important in the Allied plans for prosecution of the attack against Japan. The ring around Rabaul was growing tighter and the situation of Japan more precarious with each passing week.

General MacArthur and Admiral Kinkaid were now planning for the future. The general proposed to the Joint Chiefs of Staff that he bypass several of the Japanese bases in New Guinea and the southern islands, and seize Hollandia in Dutch New Guinea, while Admiral Halsey, acting for Admiral Nimitz, would seize Emirau Island at the same time, thus furthering the war and putting the final touches on the isolation of Rabaul. So Emirau Island was seized, but there were no Japanese there—they had left the island a few weeks earlier, seeing the handwriting on the wall.

Slowly the physical resources of Admiral Kinkaid's Seventh Fleet began to increase, but in terms of the war effort, the submarines operating out of Australia were still the most important element. There were then 24 submarines under Admiral Christie's command (as compared to 73 boats operating out of Pearl Harbor), and together with the Pearl Harbor vessels the Australia ships had sunk 30 Japanese warships and 435 merchant ships, so many of them in the Dutch East Indies area that Japan's fuel situation was becoming extremely precarious. The major reason that the Japanese had precipitated the Pacific War was to guarantee a fuel supply from the Dutch East Indies to prosecute the China War, after the Americans had cut off U.S. oil shipments in 1941. Now their situation was growing so desperate that the movement of the Combined Fleet was extremely limited, and most of that fleet was remaining in Southeast Asian waters.

Typical of the American submarines operating out of Australia was the U.S.S. *Bowfin,* which in January went out on her third war patrol from Fremantle, stopping off at Exmouth Gulf to take on all the fuel her tanks could hold. The submarine captain, Commander Walter Griffith, took her through Lombok Strait, into the Java Sea, and along the coast of Borneo. Like many of the submarines of that period, the *Bowfin* was having torpedo troubles, caused by the faulty magnetic exploders on the American torpedoes. All this was just then being unraveled at Pearl Harbor and in Washington, and ultimately it would be discovered that the seat of the trouble lay well back in American naval history—back in the days just after the end of World War I, when the Americans examined the German torpedoes and decided they were worth copying. So they did copy them and thus inherited the faulty magnetic exploder that had also troubled Admiral Doenitz in the Atlantic in the early days of World War II in Europe.

The Germans did not solve their problems until the summer of 1940 by deactivating the magnetic exploder and beginning production of new torpedoes. The American problem was still troublesome in the winter of 1943–44. That January, 1944, the *Bowfin* had been ordered to interrupt her patrol and to put in at Darwin, where it picked up Admiral Christie. The admiral wanted to go out to observe a patrol in action, to see at close range what the torpedoes could, or could not, do. They would lay mines off the Borneo coast and then go hunting for enemy ships to sink.

First they sank a 5,000-ton merchant ship, not big but worth the torpedo. The next was a cargo ship, about twice as large. Then they laid the mines off the port of Balikpapan, on the Makassar Strait.

The ravages of the submarine command against the Japanese contributed to Admiral Koga's decision, made that February, to move the headquarters of the Japanese Combined Fleet from Truk to the Palau Islands. It was part of the general retraction of Japanese defenses. The Imperial General Staff was becoming very worried about the fuel situation, particularly after February, when the *Bowfin* and the other American submarines sank fifty-three cargo ships, and the Allied airmen from Australia and the South Pacific sank another sixty-six ships. Of these, twenty-five were tankers, and the tanker situation was becoming so serious that ships already under construction in Japan were being hastily converted to become tankers.

As the Japanese moved back on their chessboard, the Allies moved forward. Admiral Lockwood was preparing to make use of Seeadler Harbor that spring and was getting ready to move the submarine tender *Eurydale* to the harbor, the first major jump in the South Pacific. Everyone, on both sides of the Pacific War, could sense that the tension was building and that the Allied Forces were beginning to move faster. The Japanese moved their major fleet elements to Tawitawi, very near the oilfields. Meanwhile General MacArthur and Admiral Kinkaid prepared to move north toward the Philippines and in May to invade Biak off the northwest coast of New Guinea. And in Washington, the Joint Chiefs of Staff prepared to straighten out a difficult command situation that had existed since the summer of 1942.

During that summer Admiral King had insisted on the invasion of Guadalcanal, although General MacArthur was not yet ready to move. And in so fighting for and winning the battle with the Joint Chiefs, Admiral King had also held out for maintaining control of the Guadalcanal operations, on the principle that if the others did not believe it was possible—as they indicated—then they were not the people to fight the battle. Thus General MacArthur's domain in the southern Pacific had been cut in two, and he had been forced to share it with Admiral Nimitz and with his Third Fleet commander, Admiral Halsey.

The U.S. Navy's war plan—Plan Orange—had always envisaged a swift defeat of the fragmentary American forces in the Pacific, followed by the difficult island-hopping drive back across the Pacific. By the spring of 1944 the Allies had captured the Gilbert Islands and the Marshalls, and were eying the Marianas. Although the navy had instituted the Guadalcanal campaign, it was not really part of the navy's plan but rather a target of necessity to save Australia.

In the spring of 1944 this fact was recognized by the Joint Chiefs of Staff, and the command situation was straightened out by giving back to General MacArthur the control of and responsibility for virtually all of the southern Pacific area. On June 15 the forces would be redisposed, and practically all of the infantry troops in the area would be put under MacArthur's command. Also, MacArthur's Navy would get a big boost. For the first time, the Seventh Fleet could really call itself a fleet, with the addition of three cruisers, twenty-seven destroyers, thirty submarines, eighteen destroyer escorts, an amphibious command ship—which would give Admiral Barbey what he needed— an attack transport, an attack cargo ship, five destroyer transports, forty LSTs, and sixty LCIs. This was truly a fleet, and the change meant that General MacArthur and Admiral Kinkaid could mount their own amphibious operations without pleading with Admiral Nimitz for ships to carry them out.

The next step for General MacArthur and Admiral Kinkaid would be to move into Dutch New Guinea, which was the obvious jump-off point for the return to the Philippines.

6

PRELUDE TO HOLLANDIA

March 12, 1944. For many months a secret battle had been raging within the American military establishment, between the army and the navy over the command and conduct of Pacific operations concerning the future American initiative. The navy wanted to push across the Central Pacific to Formosa, China, or Japan proper. The army, reflecting General MacArthur's view, wanted to move back up New Guinea and return in triumph to the Philippines. When the Joint Chiefs of Staff assessed the whole situation, at the end of 1943, a new element was brought in. The B-29 superfortress bombers, which had been developed for use in bombing Japan from long distance, were not going to be able to do the job properly from west China bases, which was the original thought. The distance was too great, and the planes could not reach the key home island of Honshū from Chengdu.

The success of the Central Pacific drive into the Gilberts and the Marshall Islands brought up the question of the Marianas, which had excellent air bases at Saipan, Tinian, and Guam, from which the superfortresses could easily reach Japan and return. So when the discussions continued among the Joint Chiefs of Staff, the army found that the army air force had gone over to the side of the navy, and that the JCS then were tending in favor of the navy's plan. General MacArthur tried to persuade the Joint Chiefs to order Admiral Nimitz to assist the general in moving into Mindanao, and he tried to downplay the navy's plan. But the Joint Chiefs did not agree. MacArthur persisted to the extent that the Joint Chiefs appointed an investigating committee representing all three services, and ultimately the committee reported in favor of the navy's plan. And so, on March 12, the Joint Chiefs spelled out the immediate future for General MacArthur and Admiral Nimitz.

The plan called for abandonment of the occupation of Kavieng, which was on General MacArthur's list for invasion, as unnecessary in view of the isolation of Rabaul. The possession of the Admiralty Islands' air bases would have the same effect.

MacArthur's next step, then, would be to occupy Hollandia in Dutch New Guinea. While MacArthur was doing so, Admiral Nimitz would be capturing Saipan, Tinian, and Guam.

And then, in the fall of 1944, General MacArthur would occupy Mindanao, with the idea of reducing and containing the Japanese in the Philippines, while the navy led the advance to Formosa. So as of March 1944, General MacArthur had lost his bid for control of the Pacific War campaign, and it seemed that he was to be relegated to a secondary role in the future.

General MacArthur did not like the prospects at all, but he set out to follow his orders.

The Japanese were suspecting an Allied movement north through Dutch New Guinea and into the southern Philippines, and they did all they could to prepare for it. As of the end of March 1944, they had sent some 350 airplanes into the three airfields around Hollandia. Until March, the Japanese fields were more or less safe from attack by the Allies, because the planes of Major General George C. Kenney's Fifth Army Air Force—particularly the fighter planes—did not have the range to hit Hollandia and return to Nadzab, their farthest forward air base on New Guinea.

But modifications were being made to P-38 fighter interceptor planes to give them longer range. And just at the end of the month Kenney sent eighty B-24 heavy bombers, escorted by nearly sixty P-38 fighters, against the three Hollandia fields. The air raid caught the Japanese completely unprepared, and most of the Japanese planes were neatly parked on the runways and taxiways. It was a scene reminiscent of the Clark Field complex in the Philippines on December 8, 1941, when the Americans had been caught by surprise and their force of B-17 bombers and fighters had been decimated on the ground. The present raid was followed a few hours later by another, and then on April 3, 100 A-20 medium-attack bombers raided the fields again. On April 5, 12, and 16, more Allied raiders came over. The result was that Japanese air power around Hollandia was completely destroyed. Later, when the official counts were made, it was discovered that 340 planes had been wrecked on the ground and another 50 had been shot down and had crashed in the jungles.

In the spring of 1944, then, General MacArthur had a navy of his own, capable of taking offensive action. Its one great disadvantage was the lack of an aircraft carrier force, but later this would be made up, in part, by the assignment of a number of escort carrier groups to the fleet.

Vice-Admiral Kinkaid now had a real fleet at his disposal. Rear Admiral Victor A. C. Crutchley commanded the cruiser force, which consisted of H.M.A.S. *Australia,* H.M.A.S *Shropshire,* and several U.S. destroyers.

Rear Admiral Russell S. Berkey had the cruisers *Phoenix, Nashville,* and *Boise,* and destroyers to screen them.

Admiral Barbey had his Seventh Amphibious Force, of transports, escorts and landing craft, and landing ships.

Admiral Kinkaid also commanded a number of service ships, motor torpedo boats, and the submarines of the Australian command, Admiral Christie's force based in

Fremantle, and Captain John M. Haines's forces based in Brisbane. And Kinkaid had an air arm, which consisted, at first, of B-24 Liberator heavy bombers and PBY Catalina flying boats. Soon, the seaplane tender *Tangier* was moored in Seeadler Harbor, and this change made it possible to fly searches 500 miles north of Manus and to conduct air raids as far as the Caroline Islands.

By March, General MacArthur had gained control of what had been the Australian sector of New Guinea—Papua—and was looking ahead to the conquest of the entire island: that meant Dutch New Guinea, about one hundred fifty thousand square miles of mountain and jungle. In the area that interested MacArthur, a four-hundred-fifty-mile stretch of coastline, there was only one harbor and anchorage worth worrying about. This was Humboldt Bay, but to the Americans the whole area came to be called Hollandia, after a little settlement at Challenger Cove, an arm of the bay. West of the bay are the Cyclops Mountains, and south of this mountain range is Lake Sentani, narrow, like America's Lake Champlain, but only fifteen miles long. There were three important airfields in this area. MacArthur was now ready to capture them and the harbor he would use for supply.

By the fourth week of March 1944, Admiral Kinkaid had drawn up his plans, which also called for the support of Task Force Fifty-eight, the carrier arm of the Pacific Fleet, and the landings at Hollandia. There were to be three separate landings, at Tanahmerah and Humboldt bays, and at Aitape.

Admiral Kinkaid would have liked nothing better than to command the invasion force himself, but General MacArthur was a hard taskmaster, who insisted that Kinkaid be available to him at all times. So Kinkaid had to turn over command of the operation to Admiral Barbey, who would direct the whole from his new command and communications ship, the *Blue Ridge*. Barbey decided to oversee the Tanahmerah landing himself, so he gave the command of the Humboldt Bay operation to Admiral William M. Fechteler, and that of Aitape to his own chief of staff, Captain Alfred G. Noble.

By the end of 1943, the Japanese were certain that MacArthur was going to try to go back to the Philippines. In fact, the Japanese high command assessed the future American strategy more shrewdly than did the Americans at that moment. They saw MacArthur's making a major advance along the north coast of New Guinea in the spring, and they began reinforcing the area. As the Allies prepared to move, the Japanese were bringing troops into the Hollandia area, also properly assessing the next American step. Their movement was not as effective as it might have been, largely because General Hatazo Adachi, the commander of the Eighteenth Army in New Guinea, dragged his feet in complying with orders to move troops immediately to Aitape. Thus, Adachi really hindered the Japanese defenses at this time.

As far as navy forces were concerned, the Japanese also had a fleet in New Guinea. It was named the Ninth Fleet, and its commander was Vice-Admiral Yoshikazu Endo. But Admiral Endo's fleet consisted of only a handful of subchasers, minelayers, and transportation barges. He did not have any cruisers or destroyers. Neither did he have many aircraft. And he could no longer count on the strong force of the army's Sixth Air Division, because of the great Allied raids of March and April. The sign of what had happened to that Japanese air force came in April, when the commander of the Sixth Air Division was relieved and sent home to Tokyo in disgrace because of the loss of those 400 badly needed airplanes.

So the Japanese knew what was coming, and early in April they ordered Major General Kitazano down to Hollandia to take charge of the defense. But General Kitazano was killed, so Lieutenant General Fusataro Teshima took command of the defenses. He had the Second Army, with headquarters on the Vogelkop Peninsula, and several new divisions.

General Teshima's orders were to hold Hollandia at all costs. These were the sort of orders that the Imperial General Headquarters was giving more and more those days, with no real belief that they could be carried out. What the Japanese high command meant was "fight to the death, and buy some more time."

The Japanese defense plan of the Hollandia area was based on the defense perimeter of the empire set up in 1943, a new line that ran through the Marianas, the Palaus, western New Guinea, and the Dutch East Indies. The talk, of course, was of building up forces behind that line, powerful attack units, which would then swoop down on MacArthur and "annihilate" him and his men.

Hollandia was supposed to become the major jump-off base for the reconquest of Papua and the Solomons, and its capture was to lead to a Japanese victory in the South Pacific. But that is not how the war was going in the spring of 1944, and the Japanese in Tokyo knew it very well. On March 25, Lieutenant General Adachi was ordered to withdraw his army from eastern New Guinea, where he had already been badly battered by MacArthur, to Hollandia to help with that defense. That was an excellent idea, but General Adachi stalled, and by mid-April only two regiments of the Eighteenth Army were starting along the jungle trails, heading for Hollandia. The Allies were on their way to that same spot, but by sea.

So, in the spring of 1944 the stage was set for the preliminary moves that would take General MacArthur back to the Philippines. The Joint Chiefs of Staff were still adhering to the concept of the drive across the Central Pacific, but General MacArthur was unwavering. He would follow his orders and await an opportunity to get his own way. Just now the step was to capture Hollandia. MacArthur and MacArthur's Navy were ready to go.

7

LANDINGS IN HOLLANDIA

B y April 20, 1944, MacArthur's Navy had really come of age. The triple-pronged attack on Dutch New Guinea was the largest undertaking MacArthur had yet tried. It involved 215 vessels, ranging from heavy cruisers to landing craft, and for cover had Task Force Fifty-eight, which meant 15 aircraft carriers. Besides this invasion force, the Seventh Fleet now had 7 escort carriers of its own for close support.

Admiral Barbey had given up his communications ship, the U.S.S. *Blue Ridge,* to ride in the destroyer *Swanson* for this invasion of Dutch New Guinea. The transports and the destroyer transports would take the men of two divisions, the Forty-first and the Twenty-fourth, to make the landings. One reinforced Regimental Combat Team of the Forty-first Division, the 163rd Infantry, would make landings at Wakde Island, one hundred twenty miles west of Aitape, but this would not occur until early May.

At 7 A.M. on the morning of April 20 the ships of the invasion force, aimed at Hollandia, assembled about fifty miles northeast of Seeadler Harbor on Manus Island. They were covered by eight escort carriers and seventeen destroyers, which, considering the state of the Japanese air and naval forces in the area, turned out to be enormous overkill. Still, there was always the chance of a Japanese submarine coming along, and one of the tasks of the escort carriers was to fly an antisubmarine patrol for the invasion fleet.

Intelligence officers had estimated that the Japanese strength at Aitape was thirty-five hundred men, which meant the Americans should expect quite a fight. They were ready for it as they headed in toward the landing beach at Aitape. The beach was about three-quarters of a mile long, in front of the village of Korakao and a mile from the important Tadji airstrip. The airstrip would offer no difficulties, since the planes were dead on the ground. The native Melanesians might offer some problems if they were helping the Japanese, but that still had to be ascertained.

The first problem was to get the landing troops in to the beach, and to do this the fleet had to run through a roadstead that consisted of four islands large enough to house Japanese shore guns. Captain Noble, who was in charge of the landing, had to assume that the guns would be there and had to count on neutralizing them with naval gunfire from the destroyers, three-inch guns, and with bombers and fighter planes from the escort carriers.

At 6 A.M. on April 21 the destroyers were coming in, firing, and they continued to fire on the four islands until 6:30. Then they stopped, while the fighter planes and bombers plastered the islands and ripped up the sand with machine-gun bullets.

The landing craft assembled three miles offshore and headed in, in nine waves. When the first wave hit the beach, the surf sank several landing craft, but most got in safely. They had expected anything, but all they experienced was sporadic rifle fire. The men began to move, and they soon found why there was so little opposition. Nearly all the troops had been service military, not infantry, and they had run inland so quickly that they had left their fires going and their breakfasts uneaten. The landings were reminiscent of those first ones on Guadalcanal in August 1942, when the Marines had surprised the Japanese engineers and construction battalions, who were building the forward airstrip there.

At Aitape, the eight following waves had virtually no opposition, and by nightfall the landing area was secure. The Americans had suffered two men killed and thirteen wounded. By noon the Australian engineers had arrived. It was their job to rehabilitate the Tadji airstrip. In two days they had it in adequate shape, and Australian P-40 fighter planes were brought in. The American aviation engineers came in, as well, and began building a bomber strip next to the fighter strip.

So at Aitape, the Allied landings had been most satisfactory.

The same could not be said for the landings at Tanahmerah Bay.

The first problem was a matter of intelligence. Neither the Americans nor the Australians knew very much about this part of Dutch New Guinea. They had maps, but the maps were not accurate. One, for example, showed a big trail which ran from the head of Tanahmerah Bay to Lake Sentani. But aerial photographs showed no signs of the trail. The submarine *Dace* landed an Australian party of scouts, but the Melanesian natives betrayed them to the Japanese, who attacked and killed four members of the party and forced the others to hide in the jungle. The *Dace* remained offshore for two days, sending signals at night to the force ashore. The signals received no replies, and after the second night the submarine returned to Seeadler Harbor. No information came back from that scouting party.

Because of this lack of real information, the whole invasion had to be planned from aerial photographs, which, unfortunately, showed nothing of the actual condition of the terrain on which the soldiers would have to move.

At 5 A.M. on April 22 the Western Attack Force came in,

preceded by the Australian cruiser force, which bombarded the area thoroughly. There was absolutely no reaction, so Admiral Barbey concluded that there were no Japanese troops in the Tanahmerah Bay area. He was right. Two regiments of the Twenty-fourth Infantry Division landed in seven waves without incident. Some scattered rifle fire and a machine gun were heard, but they died down soon enough.

The trouble, the Americans soon discovered, was not the Japanese but the terrain. Beach Red One was only a hundred yards long, and it was surrounded by coral reef. Landing craft could cross the reef for about an hour at high tide, and that was all. Only two LCM landing craft could beach at once. The water was too shallow for an LST even to try. The only solution was the use of Amphracs, which could cross the coral in shallow water.

Fortunately there was no Japanese opposition, so the troops could recover. But the lack of geographical information continued to be troublesome. The Americans came across a maze of trails that seemed to lead nowhere, but finally they sorted out one narrow trail that led toward Lake Sentani. It was so narrow and steep that only foot soldiers could use it. By nightfall foot patrols had penetrated eight miles inland without meeting any serious opposition.

Much worse was the situation at Beach Red Two. The aerial photographs had not shown that just behind this beach was a swamp that was completely impassable. There was no way to get men or equipment from the beach to firm ground. The maps had shown a road that led to this second beach, but the road did not exist. The engineers tried to build a road, but after a day and a half they had to admit that it would take more than a week to do it.

So the beach was a mess, with men and equipment piled up, going nowhere. The only solution was to take the men off Beach Red Two and move them by water to Beach Red

One. This was done. It took all day, and the tanks and other heavy equipment never did get off the beach and were abandoned there to be salvaged later.

The entire landing area was a terrible mess. To try to make some order of it, the navy brought in demolition men, who began blasting the coral reef and created a channel that ran between Depapre Inlet and Beach Red One. It took the engineers a week to make a channel 500 feet long, 60 feet wide, and 14 feet deep. Then the beach could take LSTs, and the tanks could be gotten off.

Everybody concerned was seriously embarrassed on D-Day when General MacArthur arrived at Tanahmerah Bay for a look. He came ashore, along with General Krueger, the commander of the U.S. Sixth Army, General Eichelberger, and Admiral Barbey, and they saw what a mess had been created. After an hour, MacArthur left for Aitape, much to the relief of the landing force. At conferences in the afternoon, General Eichelberger and Admiral Barbey agreed that Tanahmerah Bay had been an enormous mistake, and so the main effort was directed toward moving over to Humboldt Bay. The two regiments that had already been landed would continue to drive toward the airfields, but the rest of the expected landing force would be diverted. Nobody really counted on those two regiments left back at Tanahmerah to be much help in the fighting ahead, at least not for a while.

The third landing force of the Hollandia invasion was slated for Humboldt Bay, also on April 22. But there was one great difference. The Allies knew what they were getting into. Enough traders had come here in the past to provide some good maps and knowledge of the terrain.

South of Hollandia village lay a good beach seven hundred yards long that the Americans called Beach White One. Another beach, Beach White Two, was located on a long sand spit called Cape Tjeweri. Inside the spit was a landing called Pim, which the Japanese had used, and from Pim a road led to Lake Sentani. So for once the Allies were in luck.

The main landing was made on Beach White One, because the LSTs could come in there. One battalion was to land on Beach White Two, using Amphtracs and DUKWs in the shallow water, and head for Pim.

Before sunrise on April 22 the destroyers were offshore, and the landing craft were four miles off the beach, waiting. Three cruisers opened fire on Japanese targets in the village of Hollandia and on the beaches and places in the hills where Japanese guns were supposed to be. The aircraft carriers sent in their planes to make air strikes. The bombers laid mines and bombs in neat patterns, using intervalometers that spaced the explosives evenly along the beach.

Again, as at Aitape, the Japanese were completely surprised. The Americans found few enemy troops, for most of them had fled inland. They found cooking fires and hot food. They captured many prisoners, a very unusual state of affairs in the Pacific War. But it was true; in a few hours the Americans captured more than six hundred prisoners, and that was far more than had surrendered during the entire campaign for Guadalcanal.

By 9 A.M. the major invasion points had been captured, and an hour later General MacArthur came ashore from the cruiser *Nashville* to have a look at Beach White One. By midafternoon the troops had achieved all their D-Day objectives and stood atop the hill that dominated the village of Hollandia. By nightfall they had also taken the area around Pim landing and had linked up with the troops that landed first. And to do all this only six men had been killed. It was one of the most remarkable events of the Pacific War, coming as it did in the middle of the struggle. The only situation in any way comparable came at the very end of the war, in the battle for Okinawa, when hundreds of

Japanese surrendered—but only after they had been driven to the southern end of the island and their backs were to the sea. The Hollandia surrenders had to be credited to the extremely low morale of the Japanese troops, and this had to be attributed to their commanders, Admiral Endo and General Inada, but there was another reason. Ninety percent of the Japanese troops in this region of New Guinea were service troops, with neither the training nor the indoctrination of the front-line soldiers that the Americans had been meeting in the past.

By the end of D-Day the ship *Westralia* and 7 LSTs had landed their cargoes on Beach White One, and 4,000 tons of ammunition and other supplies were ashore. There was scarcely room for them on the narrow beach, with 300 vehicles and a major Japanese supply and ammunition dump that had been left there.

The Japanese dump was to cause plenty of trouble that night. An Allied bomber had dropped an explosive into the supply dump during the day, and the bomb started a fire. No one paid much attention at first, because no one wanted the Japanese supplies, anyhow, except for the souvenir value of some items.

Later in the day the navy saw the fires, for the one fire had spread, and tried to send a minesweeper in to put them out. But the minesweeper could not get in close enough for its hoses to play on the fires, so they burned all that night of April 22.

Just before nine o'clock that night a Japanese bomber came over to snoop on the invaders, and the pilot dropped a stick of bombs on the existing fires. More fires broke out and they soon spread to the ammunition dump. It began to blow up, and the flames spread even more. The navy then had to begin trying to evacuate troops from the beach, and so did boats of the Engineer Special Brigade. All night long they ran in and out of the shoreline, taking off troops. When morning came, they counted the casualties: More men had been killed and wounded by the exploding ammunition dump than by the Japanese. Twenty-four men were dead, and more than a hundred were wounded.

For the next four days the beach fires burned and ammunition continued to explode. When it was over, most of the rations and other supplies landed on D-Day had been destroyed. The troops had to be supplied from other areas, and LSTs had to be rammed up onto Beach White Two. On April 24 the troops of the 186th Infantry had to go on half rations because of the beach destruction.

In spite of all this seeming confusion, the American troops forged ahead in the Hollandia area. By noon of April 24 the regiment had reached Lake Sentani and there had begun to fight a concentration of Japanese troops. The airfield called Cyclops was captured on April 26, and later that day Sentani Field was taken. Tami airstrip was captured on May 1, even though the supply problem continued. For several days the troops of the 186th lived on captured Japanese supplies, which meant rice and canned fish.

The Hollandia operation came to an end successfully early in June. The Americans had suffered twelve hundred casualties, mostly wounded. The Japanese had suffered four thousand casualties.

That was the end of the amphibious phase, and the role of MacArthur's Navy ceased largely when the service troops took over. Task Force Fifty-eight was released so the carriers could participate in the coming Marianas operation. But there still was one big battle to be fought.

Early in May the U.S. Thirty-second Division, commanded by Major General William H. Gill, arrived in the Aitape area and took over from the 163rd Infantry Regimental Combat Team, which was going on to assault Wakde Island, one hundred twenty miles to the west of Aitape and one of the stops on MacArthur's road back to the Philippines. General Gill still faced the problem of the Japanese, which had not really been resolved. General

Adachi's Eighteenth Army was located at Wewak, about a hundred miles east of Aitape. Fortunately for the Allies, they captured documents that revealed that General Adachi was planning an attack on Aitape. It began to materialize in late May. General Krueger sent the Forty-third Infantry Division and two extra regiments to that area to be prepared for them. The Japanese finally launched their attack on the night of July 10.

The Japanese attacked with two divisions. They broke through the American lines, and for a while the issue was very much in doubt. So MacArthur's Navy was called back into action. On July 10 Admiral Kinkaid sent in PT boats to harry the Japanese along the coast. He also ordered the Australian cruiser force into action, which included two American destroyers, the *Ammen* and the *Bache*. For several days the cruiser force moved up and down the coast, controlling the roads that supplied General Adachi's forces and destroying his supply trains. General Adachi, though fighting valiantly, was eventually forced to withdraw because of a shortage of supplies. In mid-August he did so, having lost about half of the twenty thousand men he had thrown into the battle, while the Americans had suffered three thousand casualties, again most (twenty-six hundred) of them wounded.

8

TO THE VOGELKOP

Target: Mindanao. Target date: November 15, 1944.

This was General MacArthur's overall plan for the movement back to the Philippines. In the spring of 1944, after Hollandia, he planned four more stages of movement to achieve that end. MacArthur's Navy would carry the Southwest Pacific Forces all the way.

1. Wakde. This area, sometimes called Wakde-Sarmi, is located 120 miles west of Hollandia on the north coast of New Guinea. It was important because of the four air bases that the Japanese had built in the area.

2. Biak. One of the Schouten Islands, which lie across the top of Geelvink Bay. It had been listed by the Japanese as an important link in the defense perimeter of the empire that was established early in 1943, but in the spring of 1944 it was downgraded, and the Japanese high command began to call it an outpost. Again, this area was important for its airstrips.

3. Numfoor. Once more, this island was important for its air bases. It lies west of Biak off the Vogelkop Peninsula. Three airfields were completed in 1944.

4. Sansapoor. This was the base always wanted by General MacArthur for his drive to the Philippines. To the

Japanese it was important because the Klamono oil field was only a few miles to the southwest. The Japanese had begun this Pacific War, as noted, for the specific purpose of assuring themselves a constant supply of fuel. Borneo and the islands around Dutch New Guinea were the keys to Japanese military survival.

MacArthur's Navy was now a completely organized and competent force. Admiral Kinkaid, who had distinguished himself first as commander of cruisers at the Battle of the Coral Sea and then at Midway, had then gone on to further accomplishment in the Aleutians after the Japanese landed there in the spring of 1942. His subordinate commanders, Admirals Berkey and Crutchley, were experienced cruiser men, and Admiral Barbey, who had shown his ability to do much with few resources, had now been given many more adequate ships to work with in his Seventh Fleet Amphibious Force.

So MacArthur's Navy prepared to attack Wakde and capture the airfield and the small but important port facilities there. It was not going to be an easy task, for the Japanese had stationed their Thirty-sixth Division at Wakde, and about eleven thousand men were distributed among three major areas, around Wakde and Sarmi.

But more important than the land defenses of this part of Dutch New Guinea was something new that Admiral Kinkaid learned about in March. For a long time the Japanese naval high command had been talking about the "decisive battle" by which they hoped to defeat the American fleet and thus put a stop to the U.S. drive back across the Pacific. It had been Admiral Isoroku Yamamoto's one hope of bringing the war to a successful conclusion. Yamamoto's successor, Admiral Koga, had followed that dream as well until he was killed in a plane crash. And now Admiral Soemu Toyoda, the new commander of the Combined Fleet, had devised what was called Operation A-Go, which called for the Japanese fleet to move out to meet the next important strategic move by the Americans and the Australians against the defense line of the "Inner Empire."

General MacArthur would have liked to have kept on moving after the successful landings in the Hollandia region, but his land commanders said that they needed a respite to get ready, so the plans were delayed. The invasion of Wakde was set for May 15, 1944. Admiral Fechteler would be in command of the naval task force. By the time of the invasion, nobody in the Allied command was very happy about it, because new information showed that the whole operation might not be necessary. The thought had been that Hollandia and Wakde could be used as airfields for heavy bombers, but aerial photos showed that it was not the case. Biak was the only place on the Dutch New Guinea coast from which the heavy bombers could successfully operate, and the capture of Biak was the really important matter.

But the Wakde Operation was in the works, and it went on. The value of it would be that the Wakde-Sarmi airfields would help the effort to invade Biak a little later.

Admiral Kinkaid and General MacArthur had been asking for aircraft carriers to make their Seventh Fleet complete. But Admiral Nimitz resisted this move for several reasons, not least of which was his desire to maintain control of major fleet operations. Thus he was willing to "lend" MacArthur's Navy fleet carriers and light carriers for special operations, but he was not willing to sacrifice any of the major elements of the fleet's task force. He was right in this attitude, as was to be shown at the Battle of the Philippine Sea in a few weeks. It would have been a serious mistake to fragment the American fleet's forces.

So Admiral Kinkaid and General MacArthur had to be content with their escort carriers, although in truth they were not. For the truth was that in this period of the Pacific War no one except the few commanders who operated escort carrier groups really appreciated the strength offered by half a dozen of the small carriers working together.

So the plans continued. Wakde was to be assaulted by the 163rd Regimental Combat Team. Ten days after its assault, the rest of the Forty-first Division would move against Biak.

In the second week of May the various forces began to assemble. The 163rd Infantry Regiment had been relieved of garrison duty at Aitape and was now ready for another assault. The men got aboard the ships and landing craft and by May 16 were assembled offshore at Hollandia. The cruisers and destroyers of the covering force had already left to run up to Wakde and wait. The LSTs started moving toward Wakde.

Since about April 1, the air forces had been plastering this whole attack area with bombs, and the fighter planes had been running in on strafing raids. Biak was under almost daily attack, which was done partly to give the Japanese the impression that Biak would be the next point struck. But for three days beginning May 13, the bombers hit Wakde hard. Then on May 17 while the troops got ready to go ashore at Wakde, the bombers hit Biak again. It was a sort of guessing game from the Japanese viewpoint.

But the fact was that the Japanese were not fooled. As soon as the Americans landed at Hollandia, the Japanese high command became certain that Biak was the next important attack point. But in Tokyo this was not now so meaningful, because Japan was beset on many sides, and already the defense line established in the winter of 1943 was beginning to crack. Biak had been called a key link in the empire's defense perimeter, but on May 9 the Imperial General Headquarters announced that Biak was no longer within that perimeter.

The reason for the announcement was directly connected with the great successes of the American submarine force, particularly that part of the force stationed at Brisbane and in the Perth area. The submarines of MacArthur's Navy had been doing a really remarkable job of harrying the Japanese and picking away at their supply lines.

Since late winter the Japanese had been taking note of the increased American submarine activity by devoting more of their efforts to convoy and antisubmarine patrol. Admiral Koshira Oikawa had been appointed to command the Grand Escort force, and a large number of new ships called *kaibokan* had been given to him for the job. These *kaibokan* were patrol vessels, and they carried several hundred depth charges. Their one reason for existence was to find and sink submarines. And the new *kaibokan* units were not alone.

The Japanese had discovered the usefulness of the hunter-killer teams of ships and aircraft, just as the British and Americans had discovered, and employed, this combination in the European and Atlantic theaters. In Japan the 901st Naval Air Flotilla had been organized and assigned to Admiral Oikawa, who was working on a plan to run a mine field all the way down the Japanese defense perimeter, from Honshū to the island of Borneo.

For more than four months, Admiral Oikawa had been fighting a most discouraging battle against the Americans. With the loss of the Japanese position in Papua, New Guinea, with the defeats at Buna and Gona, and the beginning of the MacArthur drive toward Dutch New Guinea, the Japanese had decided to reinforce New Guinea and stop the Americans and Australians right there. But talk was easier than action, and even in January 1944, the sinking of tankers had created serious oil shortages in Japan. Serveral special tanker convoys had been sent up from the oil fields to relieve the situation. At the end of January one such convoy was attacked in the East China Sea by the American submarine *Tambor,* which sank two ships of the convoy. Very shortly thereafter another convoy was attacked by the submarine *Jack,* which sank four of the five tankers.

That winter it was apparent to the Imperial General Headquarters that two major areas of the Japanese defense perimeter were threatened. The Americans would obviously make a move toward the Marianas, because the islands

MACARTHUR'S NAVY

could be used for air bases for the B-29 bombers. The
Japanese knew all about that, and had known since the
beginning of production of the B-29s, one of the worst-kept
secrets of the war.

The Japanese had also expected a major assault on
northwestern New Guinea, because they knew that General MacArthur would be trying to get back to the Philippines.

So special convoy arrangements were made to protect
the supply lines to the two special areas. In the case of the
Marianas a series of convoys was set up, the *Take,* or
bamboo convoys, as they were called, and their purpose
was to put enough troops and equipment into the Dutch
East Indies to stop MacArthur's move.

The convoys were primarily an army show, although the
ships were actually protected by the navy. That was due to
the odd arrangement of the Japanese forces, by which the
army ran its own little navy, supplying and reinforcing its
army commands with ships manned by army sailors.

That spring of 1944, the Japanese sent down several
convoys of troops and supplies to reinforce the whole area.
The first two were attacked, and the losses were heavy. On
April 17, anticipating a new attack by MacArthur, the
Japanese loaded two divisions of battlewise troops at
Shanghai and sent them to western New Guinea. The
convoy was so big and so important that it was managed by
Rear Admiral Sadamichi Kajioka and had a dozen destroyers, escorts, and a large number of aircraft assigned to it for
protection. But one large transport was sunk before the
convoy ever got to Manila, carrying down a whole regiment
of troops. On May 6 the American submarine *Gurnard*
encountered the convoy—eight big transports and a score
of escorts—and attacked. Lieutenant Commander Charles
H. Andrews, the skipper of *Gurnard,* was lucky that day.
He sank three transports, and three more regiments went
into the sea. The Japanese ships rescued many of the
troops, but their equipment went to Davy Jones. The im-

pact was so serious that the Imperial General Headquarters stopped the convoy at Halmahera, because there was no point in sending a large body of disorganized units and men without equipment into a battle zone.

That is why on May 9, three days after the sinkings, the army section of the Imperial General Headquarters announced that it no longer considered the Biak area important. What the Imperial General Headquarters meant was that they had failed to reinforce the area and to supply it, and that they had no real alternative but to announce its abandonment as a line of defense.

Less than a week after receiving this confusing information, Lieutenant General Tagami, commander of the Wakde defense area, was hit by the invasion from the sea.

It was six o'clock on the morning of May 17, when the Australian-American cruiser force appeared off Wakde and Sarmi and began to bombard the shore. The bombardment lasted nearly an hour. General Tagami's troops, most of whom were service troops, were thoroughly confused and disorganized. Then came rocket-firing landing craft to soften up the beaches more and then the landing craft filled with troops. At Wakde the defense was minuscule. No Japanese aircraft appeared, and the troops ashore moved back and let the Americans get established on the beach. They captured Wakde Island, and the ships continued to shell the town of Wakde. The ships and the Japanese shore guns and machine guns at Wakde engaged in battle that afternoon and evening, and the Allied troops cleaned up Wakde Island and adjacent areas, and prepared for the assault on Wakde town.

That assault began on the morning of May 18, on the six-hundred-yard-long beach south of the jetty in the southwestern area. The bombardment began at 8:30 and the troops of the 163rd Infantry began to land in six waves at about 8:50.

Two rocket landing craft came in first and laid down a barrage on the beach. The first craft loaded with men came in three minutes later, and the Japanese, who had been waiting, opened up fire then. Two of the LCIs were hit, and several men were killed, but just after 9 A.M. the first wave hit the beach and then five more waves came in at five-minute intervals. The Japanese fought very hard, but they were hampered because they had mostly only infantry weapons and no big field guns. By 9:30 all the troops of the U.S. assault group had landed.

Thereafter the fighting was fierce but the outcome was never seriously in doubt, because nowhere in the area did the defenders have the equipment to stop the Americans. At the end of three days, the American troops had killed nearly eight hundred Japanese and had taken only four prisoners, quite a difference from Hollandia. From now on the Allies would discover the tightening of the Japanese defenses and the importance of the Imperial General Staff's exhortations to the officers and men to fight to the last.

In killing those eight hundred Japanese, the Americans had suffered forty men killed and about 100 wounded, an indication of what heavy weapons, flamethrowers and ship bombardment, and aerial support could do to keep casualties down.

After the capture of Wakde, the Americans had the airfield they wanted to house at least some heavy bombers. On May 27 the first of the B-24s came in. Soon they were blasting the road to Manila, which ran along the coast of New Guinea. The movement of General MacArthur back to the scene of his defeat was gaining impetus.

9

SURPRISE AT BIAK

Rear Admiral William M. Fechteler was in command of the amphibious element of MacArthur's Navy that was scheduled to carry out the attack on Biak. In the middle of May 1944, as the planning came to an end and the operational phase began, he did not know it, but he was in for a very big surprise.

From the beginning of the Dutch New Guinea operations, the Allied high command had begun wondering just when the Japanese navy would show itself. The Allies did not know, of course, that the Japanese defense plan had been changed again since 1943 and that Biak had now been placed by the army outside the defense line, simply because the army had failed to reinforce it and could not guarantee its survival.

But, since the Americans did not know the Japanese defense plan of 1943, they were unaware of the enormous retrenchment in Japanese thinking, and so the planning for Biak went on as if it would be stoutly defended and as if the Imperial Navy might make a move. That was why Admiral Kinkaid and General MacArthur still pressed for the aircraft carriers they could not have on a permanent basis.

The importance of Biak was far greater than that of the other areas captured in the past few months. It is one of the

Schouten Islands that lie in Geelvink Bay. He who controlled Geelvink Bay and the Schoutens could control the Vogelkop, the peninsula at the top of New Guinea that points past Halmahera and Morotai, straight at the heart of the Philippines.

Biak was especially important because of its size (twenty miles wide and forty-five miles long) and because the Japanese had built three airstrips on the island's coastal plain.

The place chosen for the landing was Bosnik, on the bay side of the island, and it was selected because it was the flattest area and because there was less jungle and swamp behind it than anywhere else on the island. Bosnik also had the biggest settlement. It had been the administrative center for the Dutch and now was the army center for the Japanese, because it did have port facilities, even if artificial ones, created by two stone jetties that crossed the reef to reach deep water.

Aerial photographs and scouting information told Admiral Fechteler that the Japanese had a number of artillery pieces and antiaircraft guns in this area, particularly around the port and the three airstrips. So he planned a heavy preinvasion naval bombardment of the whole landing zone. The cruisers *Boise, Phoenix,* and *Nashville* would carry out the bombardment with their six-inch guns. They would be supported by several destroyers, which would give troop support.

Before the landings, the land-based air forces in the area began smashing Biak with bombs. Some bombers came from the Thirteenth Air Force, now located in the Admiralty Islands, and some came from the Nadzab base in New Guinea. Some came from as far away as Darwin, and some from as close as Hollandia. Heavy B-24 bombers and A-20 medium-attack bombers ranged across the island every day. The fighter planes that covered the bombers came from Wakde, which illustrated the importance of its capture.

After a few days of this activity the island commander, Colonel Naovuki Kuzume, knew that his island was about to be invaded. He had ten thousand troops on Biak, although the Allies underestimated the strength and put it at about 20 percent of that number.

The shallow water there made it imperative to use shallow-draft craft, so the troops were assigned to ride in LSTs and be delivered to shore by LVTs and DUKWs. The engineers would be landed very quickly, and they were told that their task was to create beaching points for supply vessels. Mostly this would mean blasting channels through the coral from deep water to the shore.

On May 25, 1944, the men of the Forty-first Division boarded the ships at Humboldt Bay. The ships sailed that evening, and the next morning they were joined by the cruisers and destroyers.

The Americans were going in to face a very tough defense, although they did not know it. The Japanese defense force on Biak had been planned at a time when the island was still central to the empire's defense perimeter, and the 222nd Imperial Army Infantry Regiment had been brought down to Biak from China, where it had been in an almost constant state of battle with the China Expeditionary Force. Colonel Kuzume had tanks, plenty of artillery, and a very tough naval special landing force of 1,500 men under Rear Admiral Sadatoshi Senda.

After the Imperial General Headquarters' decision of May 9 that placed Biak outside the empire's defense line, Colonel Kuzume was informed that he was expected to fight to the last man, and that he could not expect any help. His task was to delay the enemy's use of the Biak airfields just as long as he could do so.

So the colonel prepared for a last-ditch stand near one of the airstrips, at Mokmer, where a ridge behind the airfield and the village provided a strong natural defensive position.

The defenses at Biak were to be a warning of things to come in the Pacific campaign. The colonel placed his artillery's five- and six-inch guns on the beach for initial defense against the landings. The secondary defense was located on a coral ledge behind the airfield and on the ridge behind the village. This consisted of trenches and fortified positions, with antiaircraft guns and smaller field guns, and automatic weapons and mortars, all well dug in. And then, north of these defenses was a series of limestone caves, which were roomy enough to shelter thousands of men. These caves were connected by tunnels and trenches.

Early on the morning of May 27 the Allied attack force arrived off Biak, coming up at the slow speed of eight knots, because the LSTs were towing the LCTs that would lumber across the reef to deposit men and tanks and trucks. At 6:30 that morning the naval bombardment began. The cruisers began firing the six-inch guns at the major defenses on the ridge line, and the destroyers fired their three-inch guns at targets on the beaches.

The weather was overcast but so calm that the water was like glass. The aerial and naval bombardments raised a wave of smoke above the island, but at about 7:00 A.M. it began to blow off a bit when a light east wind sprang up.

The first Allied casualties were naval. The destroyer U.S.S. *Hutchins* moved in close to the deep-water line to fire on boats in the harbor area and was in turn fired upon by one of the five-inch shore guns. A shell hit the foremast, and although the shell did not explode, it smashed through the radar room, creating a four-foot hole in the deck, and wounding three men on its way. The destroyer retired out of range and was replaced by the U.S.S. *Bache,* which fired on the gun position. The Japanese gunners fired back but missed. The *Bache* may have knocked out the gun, or it may have been done by the *Hutchins,* which came back to the beach after the casualties were cared for and the damage to the ship temporarily repaired.

If the shore gun was knocked out, it was only temporarily, because later it continued to fire and bother the invaders.

Meanwhile the air forces were doing their job, hitting the beach defenses and the ridge line and Bosnik town with bombs and strafing.

More than a hundred B-24 heavy bombers and scores of B-25 medium bombers and A-20 medium-attack bombers also circled the island, ready to strike any position on call.

The LSTs came up close to the line of departure and the LVTs were launched. Now the problem was the smoke, which was blowing out onto the invaders and obscured the sight of the beach. The Japanese added to the confusion by firing steadily with their shore guns as the invaders came in with machine guns and mortars. Rocket craft answered the fire and silenced some of the automatic weapons.

The first wave of American troops hit the beach at about 7:20 that morning, and others followed right along. But where?

Not on the nice sandy beach that they had expected to hit. They had been caught in a current of about three knots offshore, and the landing craft had drifted, so that the first wave came in to a mangrove swamp two miles west of the landing beach. Five waves landed in the wrong places, until the landing officer, Commander Dwight H. Day, was able to locate the jetties through the smoke and send the sixth wave into the right position. After that the landings went more smoothly, and very little opposition was discovered in the jetty area. By dusk 12,000 troops, a dozen tanks, two dozen field pieces, and 500 trucks and jeeps had been landed, and so had most of the supplies needed to sustain the troops ashore for the next few days.

Those first waves of troops in the mangrove swamp began making their way out to reach the coastal road. There was some delay when one regiment that had landed in the wrong place, the 186th Infantry, had to pass through another, the 162nd, in order to reach its assigned objectives. But this was done with relatively little confusion, and by the end of the day the 186th had reached its destination. The Japanese were still not much in evidence except for some sporadic machine-gun and mortar fire and the fire of the shore guns against the ships and landing forces.

By late afternoon the landing was secure, and the LSTs had come in to facilities prepared by the engineers and were discharging the rest of the cargo.

Four Japanese fighter planes appeared over the beach-head that afternoon and made a few runs and did a little strafing, but that was the entire air opposition in the early hours. Later in the afternoon two fighter bombers attacked the LSTs at the western jetty and dropped three small bombs on *LST-456*, but the bombs did not explode. Later the sailors found that the bombs had not been armed. The crewmen threw the bombs over the side of the ship.

At dusk four twin-engined bombers came in to attack, but two of them were shot down and one flew away, smoking. The fourth was hit by antiaircraft fire and tried to make a crash dive into Admiral Fechteler's flagship, the destroyer *Sampson*. The plane passed close over the bridge and struck the water just beyond the ship. It cartwheeled and smashed into the subchaser *SC-99*, then burst into flame. The burning gasoline caused serious fires on the sub-chaser. Soon they were extinguished with the help of the tug *Sonoma*, which brought its fire hoses into play. Two men were killed and eight wounded in this incident.

Altogether the landings went very well. So by the end of the day the beachhead at Biak was secure and Admiral Fechteler turned over control of the operation to Major General Horace Fuller of the Forty-first Division. Another operation of MacArthur's Navy had been successful, and without any real opposition from the Japanese navy.

In the next few days, the troops cleared up the area around the airfields. The fighting on the ground was fierce, but the might of the Americans slowly moved the Japanese out of their trenches, their blockhouses, and finally their caves. One by one the enemy artillery pieces were silenced. By the end of May air-force units were beginning to arrive, and as June began, Colonel Kuzume's forces were beginning to unravel. The attempt to slow the pace of the Americans had not been very successful, it seemed.

But now something happened that had not occurred before during the New Guinea operations of MacArthur's Navy. It had been a year since anyone in that navy had seen a Japanese ship bigger than a barge, but on June 1 came reports of Japanese naval movement down toward Halmahera, and on June 2 came an extensive air raid from carrier types of planes. It seemed that something was about to happen in New Guinea.

10

A FORAY OF THE COMBINED FLEET

The basic Japanese defense plan of 1943 called for the Combined Fleet to be prepared at any propitious moment to engage and defeat the American fleet. To streamline the fleet and make the action easier, the Japanese reorganized it, renaming the old striking force the First Mobile Fleet, and placing Vice-Admiral Jisaburo Ozawa in command. Since Ozawa was already the commander of the First Striking Force, or carrier fleet, this change put the command of the fleet under a carrier admiral.

The Combined Fleet had been commanded by an air admiral, too, but only in the broadest sense. Admiral Yamamoto had been a carrier man, a pilot, but Vice-Admiral Chuichi Nagumo, who had commanded the First Striking Force in the early days of the war, was not. Nagumo had had his training in battleships and had been assigned to the carrier fleet by Tokyo, not by Yamamoto. Nagumo did not understand carriers and their use. He was more worried about losing a carrier than using it to its fullest potential. Consequently the Japanese lost the chance to really wipe out the American fleet at Pearl Harbor, and to do the same to the British at Trincomalee.

This new Japanese battle commander, Admiral Ozawa, was not an aviator, but he understood the use of carriers better than anyone else left in the Japanese navy. After Admiral Nagumo had failed to take full advantage of his opportunities against the Americans at Pearl Harbor, at Trincomalee, and in the several air battles in the Solomon Islands area, Admiral Yamamoto had engineered not only Nagumo's downfall late in 1942 but also the promotion of Admiral Ozawa to command the striking force. After Admiral Yamamoto's death, the appointment had remained under Admiral Koga, the successor in command of the Combined Fleet.

Thus when Admiral Ozawa became commander of the actual fleet, the Japanese had an advantage over the Americans, in that Admiral Spruance, commander of the U.S. fighting fleet (the Fifth), had been a battleship admiral, a man whose essential conservatism would prevent him from taking risks. When Admiral Halsey commanded what was then the Third Fleet, a carrier admiral was in charge.

For the fleet's support of invasion operations, Admiral Nimitz had appointed Admiral Spruance, and Spruance took the most narrow view of his responsibilities. He insisted that the carrier force remain in close support of the invading amphibious fleet, even though the fleet had several groups of escort carriers that were perfectly capable of doing that job. This failure of the Americans to recognize that the carrier was the principal naval weapon of the war would lead to a great lost opportunity in June, when the Americans attacked the Mariana Islands.

In May, the Japanese were definitely looking for the opportunity for a fleet carrier battle. Admiral Shimada, the naval chief of the general staff, called that spring for surprise operations against the Americans to break their spirit. He was thinking about the New Guinea operations and suggested that the time to engage the fight was when the Americans moved into waters near the positions occupied by the Mobile Fleet.

Generally speaking, that meant, or seemed to mean, the waters around New Guinea and the Philippines, because most of the Japanese Mobile Fleet was located at Tawitawi, an island base between the Sulu and the Celebes seas, southwest of Mindanao in the Philippines and east of Borneo. This excellent protected anchorage had the great virtue, from the Japanese point of view, of being very close to the oil fields of Tarakan on Borneo.

On May 3, Admiral Toyoda, the new commander of the Combined Fleet and chief of naval operations, anticipated that the battle would be fought in the Palau Islands area, but that also included New Guinea waters, which was where the Japanese wanted to fight—very close to their fuel supply. There was also another reason: While the American carrier force had been increasing month after month, the Japanese had never recovered from the Battle of Midway, in which they had lost four important carriers. Their building program had not yet produced even one completely new carrier since the beginning of the war. Several were on the way, but they had not yet been completed, because Japanese resources simply would not permit this much activity in shipbuilding. So the Japanese planned to rely on land-based airplanes to augment the carrier force. The Japanese aircraft factories were turning out plenty of planes each month to meet the needs of both army and navy, but the pilot-training program, like shipbuilding, had never recovered from the disaster at Midway, either. The Japanese navy had been unable to change gears and bring about a program that produced trained carrier pilots and trained fighters quickly. These were the deficiencies. The positive elements for the Japanese were an enormous reservoir of men willing to make any sacrifice, and an excellent air intelligence system, really superior to that of the Americans.

In the second week of May 1944, the principal elements of the Mobile Fleet, including three carriers, lay in Lingga Roads, just south of the Malay Peninsula. Eventually it moved down to Tawitawi, while two other elements of the fleet, which included six carriers, sailed from Japan, also for Tawitawi. Thus the Imperial Navy was moving into position to challenge any further American invasions.

After the Americans had captured Hollandia, they discovered a copy of the current Japanese plan of operations, called the Z Plan, which called for movement against the American fleet at the moment of a new invasion in the Philippine Sea or along the coast of northern New Guinea. That was at the end of April. Five days later, on May 5, Admiral Toyoda had taken over the fleet and had revised the plan, which he now called Operation A-Go. Under it, the priorities were shifted away from an invasion of New Guinea and toward an invasion of either the Philippines or the Marianas.

Admiral Kinkaid had taken the Z Plan in hand, and he set out to find out what it all meant. Tawitawi had been mentioned, and so Kinkaid conferred with Admiral Christie, the submarine commander of MacArthur's Navy, who then ordered Commander Thomas W. Hogan to take the submarine *Bonefish* to Tawitawi for a look. On the night of May 14 Commander Hogan encountered a convoy of destroyers and tankers, and sank one of the destroyers. At noon the next day, still in the area, he saw several Japanese ships, including a carrier, steaming toward Tawitawi. A few hours later other sources indicated that there were six carriers in the anchorage.

As noted, the Japanese army had already declared Biak to be of no further importance, and had even refused to augment the air forces in the area. But when the Americans invaded on May 27, the navy took an entirely different view. The next day the navy sent down ninety more aircraft to join the Twenty-third Air Flotilla at Sorong, not far from Biak. Three days later another fifty-six planes were sent down to Sorong and Halmahera. The Combined Fleet had decided that it would go to the relief of Biak, and thus draw out the American fleet for the "decisive battle."

Since the army had decided against relieving Biak, no army transports were available in the area. The largest ship was the equivalent of an American LST. The Imperial Navy, then, decided that army troops would be transported in destroyers, as they had been at Guadalcanal. The plan was called Operation Kon. The troops would embark at Zamboanga in the southern Philippines and would land at Biak on June 3. Some twenty-five hundred soldiers would be moved, and they would be protected by the battleship *Fuso* and three cruisers, plus more destroyers. Air cover would come from land-based planes. The newly augmented Twenty-third Air Flotilla would attack Allied warships from the air. By the end of May more than a hundred and sixty new planes were on the way to the area, and on June 2 when eight Allied LSTs arrived at Biak from Hollandia, they came just in time to be attacked by a force of nearly sixty Japanese planes. The weather at Hollandia and Wakde was terrible and all flights had been canceled that day, so the Americans at Biak had no air cover. But they did have antiaircraft guns set up, and they used them. The Japanese attacked for more than an hour. So effective were the American antiaircraft gunners that the enemy was driven off, with only one success—a near miss of a bomb on *LST-467*, which did some damage. And for that, the cost to the Japanese air force was a dozen of the attacking planes.

Meanwhile, the Japanese reinforcements were on their way from Zamboanga. The hope in Tokyo was that the Japanese naval forces would swoop down on the un-suspecting Americans like wolves on a band of sheep, but it was foiled by an observation plane from Wakde, which sighted elements of the Japanese fleet led by Admiral Naomasa Sakonju in the cruiser *Aoba*. Sakonju reported to Tokyo that he was being shadowed by American planes, and Admiral Toyoda at the same time had an independent report of at least one carrier near Biak. He knew that these days where there was one carrier there were usually more, and so in a complete reversal, Toyoda called off the whole operation, and the troops were unloaded at Sorong. But the Japanese air elements continued their attack on Biak and the Allied ships in the vicinity.

On June 3 the Japanese airmen attacked the Bosnik area and found three American destroyers there: the *Mustin,* the *Reid,* and the *Russell.* The *Reid* was chased by Japanese planes until she finally escaped into the cover of a rain squall. She was hit repeatedly by strafing attacks and had some near misses by small bombs; one man was killed and five were wounded. The *Mustin* was later attacked but suffered no damage, nor did the *Russell.* But *LCT-248* was strafed and two men were injured before the air attack was ended by the arrival of Allied planes, which drove off the Japanese.

At this time Admiral Kinkaid was sure that the Japanese fleet was going to attack his Biak operations, and he assembled MacArthur's Navy to fight. The cruisers of Admirals Crutchley and Berkey were ordered to patrol around Biak at night. Admiral Crutchley was in command of the cruisers *Australia, Boise, Phoenix, Nashville,* and fourteen destroyers.

On June 4 the Crutchley force was spotted by Japanese planes one hundred twenty miles east of Biak, and soon navy planes came to attack. The American ships turned into an antiaircraft defense formation and fought. The cruiser *Nashville* was damaged by one near miss, but that was all. Just after midnight on the morning of June 5 the Japanese sent in torpedo bombers. They tried to sink the cruisers but missed. More effective was a Japanese air attack on the airfield at Wakde, which was crowded with Allied planes.

The Allies had become overconfident because in the last few operations they had not encountered Japanese air opposition, and they did not believe that there were many Japanese planes in the whole area. Therefore they were careless about security in parking their aircraft. The planes

sat, wing tip to wing tip, on the edges of the runway, for the
Americans had not expected any Japanese reaction. Two—
only two—bombers came over and made hash of the planes
and the airfield. Wakde Field was unusable for several
days, and about 60 of the 100 Allied planes there were
destroyed in this one foray.

That was all very well, but the destruction had not
brought about the reinforcement of Biak, and that had
been the intent. So on June 6, having ascertained that
there were no American carriers or major fleet elements in
the area, the Japanese made another attempt to save Biak.
They sent six destroyers and two cruisers to the Vogelkop.
The destroyers then moved into Sorong, and three of them
picked up about six hundred Japanese troops, while three
others covered them. They sailed for Biak at midnight on
June 7.

Admiral Crutchley's cruiser force was at sea, and Admiral Kinkaid ordered them to stand off the northeast coast of
Biak. On June 8 planes from the field at Wakde were able
to get into the air again, and they located the six Japanese
destroyers. The B-25s attacked at noon. They sank one
destroyer, the *Harusame,* and damaged another seriously.
The five destroyers then rescued the crew of the *Harusame*
and went on toward Biak. When the Japanese sighted
Admiral Crutchley's strong force of cruisers, however, they
decided to turn back.

That night, a PBY night search plane spotted the
Japanese and reported to Admiral Crutchley. The Allied
ships prepared to attack, but the Japanese turned and ran
away from the superior Allied force. The Allied ships gave
chase. The Japanese had been towing barges full of troops
and these were cast off. The Americans fired on them in
passing but kept after the Japanese destroyers, and soon
were making thirty-five knots in their chase. Behind them
came the Allied cruisers at about twenty-nine knots.

But the Japanese ran fast, and so Admiral Crutchley had
to give up chasing with his cruisers, leaving the job to the

destroyers. He went back to find and destroy the Japanese barges. The destroyers continued the chase and did get close enough to fire on the Japanese destroyer *Shiratsuyu,* but the ship kept moving, and ultimately all of the Japanese vessels escaped.

Some of the troops on the barges managed to get ashore, but not in sufficient number or with enough equipment to make much difference to the Allies.

The Japanese ships retired to their bases. The attempt to reinforce Biak had not succeeded. And now came word that changed everything, just as Admiral Toyoda was preparing to commit more and much heavier forces to the battle for Biak. Toyoda had planned to send down Vice-Admiral Matome Ugaki, once Yamamoto's chief of staff, with the battleships *Yamato* and *Musashi,* two heavy cruisers, a light cruiser, and three destroyers, escorting six cruisers and destroyers filled with troops for Biak. Ugaki was to engage any Allied ships in battle and then bombard Biak and the area. But on June 11 Pacific Fleet carrier planes began a heavy attack on Saipan, presaging the invasion of the Mariana Islands, which the Imperial General Staff also expected, and Guam. So on the night of June 12, Admiral Toyoda abruptly reversed himself, cancelled Operation Kon for the time being, and called for the beginning of Operation A-Go, which would bring on the Battle of the Philippine Sea.

After the failure of Operation Kon, the Japanese made several more attempts to reinforce Biak by barge. General Anami ordered Colonel Kuzume to prolong the defense to the last, and the colonel did so. He moved his men into the caves on the ridge and held out there. The process of dislodging the Japanese was so slow and painful that an impatient General Krueger relieved General Fuller and brought in General Eichelberger, his troubleshooter, to take over. But that did not solve the problem; every cave had to be blasted or burned out. The work on Mokmer airfield was suspended and stayed that way. It could not begin as long as the Japanese held out. And that situation lasted until June 20. So the Japanese had done as they were told. They had delayed the use of the airfields after the apparent capture of Biak, for nearly a month.

Further, the Japanese had indicated the sort of defense they were prepared to offer, now that the line of the Inner Empire had been breached. Every step the Allies took from this point on was going to be contested all the way, no matter how uselessly. The junior officers in the field had realized since spring that the war was going very badly, and they had begun making appeals to the Japanese higher authority to that effect. Higher authority, from General Tojo, the military dictator, on down, had responded with a will, for the thinking matched their own. In recent weeks the number of "suicide" attacks had increased—incidents of Japanese pilots turning their stricken aircraft to crash a ship or another plane, and incidents of soldiers in the field trying to take as many of the enemy with them as they could when they died with a grenade.

Such attacks were called *kesshi,* or daring-to-die, and they were a bit different. The pilot or the soldier would make the decision before he was hurt. Still these were individual decisions, made in the heat of battle. They were an extension of the Bushido code reengendered in Japan by Tojo in 1941.

"A sublime sense of self-sacrifice must guide you throughout life and death. . . . Do not fear to die for the cause of everlasting justice. Do not stay alive in dishonor. Do not die in such a way as to leave a bad name behind you."

That was the code of the old Samurai warriors, of the days of the shogunate and before, who got up from their sleeping mats every morning prepared to die rather than face dishonor. But now MacArthur's Navy was about to meet another fearsome weapon, which was just then being forged in Tokyo, the weapon of suicidal attack as a policy, not just as a last resort. Three months earlier Tojo had ordered the army air force to prepare to launch suicide missions, and although no one on the Allied side yet knew it, the first instance of "policy suicide" had already oc-curred, on May 27, when that cartwheeling plane had tried to crash into Admiral Fechteler's flagship and instead had ended up smashing into *Subchaser-99*. That fierce attack had been an indication of what was going to come along all too soon.

11

NUMFOOR

Even after the invasion of Biak, General MacArthur was still looking for airfield sites in New Guinea. The reason was simple enough. Planning the invasion of the Philippines, the Americans were aware of not only the strength of the Japanese army and naval air forces throughout the Philippine archipelago, but also of the "pipeline" of air defense, which was provided to the Japanese by the existence of many islands between the homeland and the Philippines. The Americans would have to be able to send hundreds of planes north to counter this defense.

West of Biak lies the island of Numfoor, and once more, its value to the Allies was that the Japanese had built up three airfields at the settlements of Kamiri, Kornasoren, and Namber. Even as the difficulties with Biak continued early in June, General MacArthur ordered the seizure of Numfoor. The decision was made in MacArthur's usual fashion: He considered the idea, sought some advice from his staff, and then acted as he pleased. People outside his staff were sometimes troubled because of a certain lordly atmosphere at Southwest Pacific command headquarters. But MacArthur had his reasons; the trouble at Biak threatened to slow him down, therefore Numfoor must be taken very quickly. Admiral Fechteler and his staff had come into Sydney aboard the command ship *Blue Ridge* and were enjoying some leave. But three days later, on June 14, the general issued his order: Numfoor by June 30.

They could not even get the *Blue Ridge* ready and up to New Guinea in time, so Admiral Fechteler and his staff flew up to Cape Sudest and took over the transport *Henry T. Allen* as command ship. On June 20 Fechteler arrived at General Krueger's headquarters to make the plans. It was impossible; no one could get ready by June 30. So General MacArthur was informed, and he agreed to a three-day delay. July 2 would be invasion day.

The 168th Infantry Regiment would lead the assault, but the 168th was just then fighting on Wakde. So the Sixth Infantry Division had to be moved to Wakde to relieve the 168th.

General Krueger made one mistake: He sent a landing party to Numfoor in a PT boat. The idea was to scout the territory for intelligence about the terrain. But the scouts were immediately detected by the Japanese and had to run. They came back with no information but had given the Japanese some important intelligence. The Americans and Australians had gone ashore near Kamiri, the site of the most important airstrip. So after the boggled scouting party, the Japanese knew what was coming and tried to prepare accordingly. They knew that the Allies were planning an attack, so they strewed the beach at Kamiri (where the scouts had gone) with land mines. They placed obstacles on the beach, and they arranged their machine guns and mortars so that they had proper fields of fire.

If the Japanese needed any further information, they got it when the Allied air forces began daily strikes on Numfoor on June 20. The two thousand Japanese defenders then spent much of their time undercover, which did not help their already sagging morale. The Japanese there had been suffering from the effects of General MacArthur's recent moves. The barges had not been coming in, and they were short on rations and needed ammunition.

The Japanese, therefore, started to save their ammunition. The Allied air forces hit the Kamiri airstrip repeatedly but received very little antiaircraft fire. There was no air opposition at all, because the planes from this area had all been sent north to fight at Saipan, where Vice-Admiral Spruance had launched the invasion of the Marianas, and the Japanese fleet had come forth to contest it in the Battle of the Philippine Sea.

The troops were brought up by Admiral Barbey in LCMs and LCTs. They were covered by the cruiser group of MacArthur's Navy, now consolidated under Commodore John A. Collins of the Australian navy. The cruiser force was stronger than it had been in the past; fourteen new destroyers had been added since the last operation. The job was to bombard all the enemy installations on Numfoor and soften it up for the July 2 landings.

The weather on D-Day was fair, with a light breeze, and the visibility was good for the aircraft that covered the operation all day long. The cruisers began their bombardment at dawn, guided by spotters in the planes overhead. The Japanese did not react except to fire at the planes occasionally with the antiaircraft guns around the airstrip.

The landings were fairly easy. The LCIs could come right into the beach through breaks in the coral reef. The LSTs brought the vehicles and tanks up to a point near the edge of the reef and then transferred them to LVTs for the landings. Two battalions of troops came in to land at once. When they landed they found almost no opposition. The bombardment and the aerial strafing of days past had been very effective, and the defenders were largely in a state of shock. Methodically the troops moved up the island and fanned out, checking every pillbox, trench, and gun emplacement. Most of these were deserted, but a few Japanese fought back, and these were quickly killed. By dusk the whole invasion force of about seventy-five hundred men had been landed. The casualties were remarkably light. One field gun in the middle of the island had fired at the beginning of the landings and had destroyed two vehicles and killed one man before the guns of the ships were turned on it and destroyed it. By the beginning of the second day the engineers were at work on the airstrip. But for some reason somebody decided that a show ought to be made. And that show brought a minor disaster.

Earlier the 503rd Parachute Infantry Regiment had been shipped to the Southwest Pacific. General Krueger decided to employ it in this operation. On the second day the First Battalion of the 503rd was flown up to Numfoor in transport planes and made an air jump onto the airfield. It was spectacular—all those parachutes floating down—but it was also a tactical mess, because many of the pilots of the transports were inexperienced, and they dropped the troops from too low an altitude. Thus the paratroopers suffered seventy-two casualties, none of them from enemy action. On July 4, the Third Battalion was flown in and dropped. This battalion suffered fifty-six casualties, again none from enemy action. So the Second Battalion was brought in by ship and had no casualties.

By the Fourth of July the Japanese were herded into an area south of Kamiri. And here they provided the fireworks for the night celebration with a series of banzai attacks. By the morning of July 5 it was all over, and most of the Japanese were dead. The 158th Regimental Combat Team sent in its Second Battalion, the last of the paratroopers arrived, and Kamiri and Namber airstrips were consolidated and in Allied hands. The Japanese who were still alive had fled into the hills, where they remained and were hunted down, until by the middle of August they were all dead or captured.

In that summer of 1944 the planning for the Pacific War took on a new urgency. General MacArthur was moving more swiftly in New Guinea than might have been expected. The invasion of the Marianas in June meant that the B-29s would be operating in a very few months and that the war against Japan would be stepped up.

In June 1944, the Allies crossed the English Channel and began the Second Front in Europe, which meant that more naval resources could be freed for the Pacific. The Joint Chiefs of Staff were now looking forward to the invasion of the Palau Islands (the site of the headquarters of the Combined Fleet). At the same time General MacArthur would attack Halmahera, which had replaced Rabaul as the center of Japanese activity in the area south of the Philippines.

For this invasion, General MacArthur wanted as many airfields in the Vogelkop area as he could manage, and he was still looking for some more. He had been talking about Waigeo, an island thirty miles northwest of the Vogelkop, but when the submarine S-47 made a scouting trip to Waigeo, the experts discovered that there were no adequate sites for an airfield there.

The general had also been talking about the Klamono oil field, which was south of the Vogelkop. Its great advantage seemed to be that the oil there was pure enough to use to fuel a ship, even if high in sulfur content (which was very hard on turbines). Oil rigs and processing equipment had been made ready in California for the Klamono field, but now the war was moving so rapidly and the services of supply were so adequate that Klamono no longer seemed so attractive; soon it was to be forgotten altogether.

The S-47 was diverted to the northeastern coast of New Guinea, and to the villages of Sansapoor and Mar, just west of the northern end of New Guinea. The scouts spent a week looking over the area, and when they came back to MacArthur's headquarters, he decided that Sansapoor and Mar would do just fine. So the invasion was ordered for July 30.

Admiral Fechteler was at sea on July 4, involved in the Numfoor operation, when he first learned that there would be a new landing in just over three weeks. He hurried back to Hollandia to confer with General Krueger at his new headquarters there.

After a spate of activity, the plans were ready on July 15, and the ships were made ready for still another landing.

There were plenty of good beaches in the Sansapoor region for a change. And, as far as scouting parties could discover, and they tried hard, there were no Japanese around these particular areas. The landing force sailed on July 27: five destroyer transports and nineteen LCIs, eight LSTs, and various other ships, escorted by eleven destroyers.

The troops landed in six waves, all within an hour, on July 30, and there was no opposition at all. By five-thirty that evening all of the ships were unloaded and started heading back to Wakde to pick up more supplies and equipment. The next day another landing was made a few miles away. They did find a few documents, which indicated that the Japanese were moving out of this whole area. East of Sansapoor, the Americans found some enemy troops and fought them. The Japanese were quickly beaten, and most of them were killed. After that there was virtually no action at all, on the ground or in the air. Not until the end of August did any Japanese planes appear in the sky.

As of the last day of August 1944, the Allied casualties in this operation were thirty-five men killed, eighty-five wounded, and nine men dead from typhus, which had broken out on the beachhead during the early days of the invasion.

And so the New Guinea operations came to an end. General MacArthur had moved from Brisbane to Port Moresby, and from Port Moresby up the east coast of New Guinea in a few short months, a distance of more than a thousand miles. The next target would be Morotai in the Halmahera Islands.

12

THE FOCUS CHANGES

In the summer of 1944, General MacArthur increased his efforts to persuade the Joint Chiefs of Staff that the impetus of the Pacific War should be changed: The focus should be moved from the Central Pacific drive, which was in the hands of Admiral Nimitz, and control should be given to General MacArthur. Admiral King was in favor of invading Formosa and the coast of China as steps to then drive on Japan itself. The Joint Chiefs of Staff were divided.

One factor favored General MacArthur and his plans to return to the Philippines: In a desperate effort to end the Pacific War by defeating China, and thus eliminating the major cause of the war from the Allied point of view, General Tojo had begun a powerful new drive to cut off east China from the wartime capital at Chongqing. Tojo hoped to squash Chiang Kai-shek, then offer peace to the Allies. He really believed they would accept it because he felt that Allied aid to China was the real cause of the Pacific War. As General MacArthur was moving up the Vogelkop in New Guinea, the Japanese army was moving south in China from Hankow toward Hanoi. The airfields in east China used by the American Fourteenth Air Force were cut off. Guilin and Guiyang were threatened. It seemed apparent that the Japanese drive would succeed, partly because Generalissimo Chiang Kai-shek was reluctant to commit the forces necessary to stop it, because this would weaken his position against the Chinese Communists by committing troops against the Japanese.

It appeared likely, therefore, that one of the best arguments of Admiral King, that the Allies could land on the China coast and be greeted by Chinese friends, was now about to be invalidated.

In the middle of July a new element entered the strategic picture. Franklin D. Roosevelt had just been nominated for an unprecedented fourth term as President of the United States. The nomination had great support—but it also had considerable public opposition, not just from the Republicans, but from many traditionalists, who had begun to believe—or said they believed—that President Roosevelt was trying to establish a lifetime rule in defiance of the two-term Presidential tradition established by George Washington. Roosevelt was concerned about this movement. Some Republicans and others were suggesting that the best possible candidate to beat Roosevelt was General Douglas MacArthur.

With these political matters hanging in the air, Roosevelt decided to make a trip to Pearl Harbor, partly for the political purpose of showing his concern for the war, and partly to discover for himself what course to pursue next in the Pacific. He had heard through Admiral William D. Leahy, his naval aide and chief of staff to the Joint Chiefs of Staff, of the quarrel between the navy and the army about the direction that the war should take in late 1944.

And so, in July 1944, General MacArthur was summoned from Brisbane to Pearl Harbor.

MacArthur interrupted his war to make a trip to Pearl Harbor for the purpose of meeting President Roosevelt and getting a decision on the conduct of the Pacific War. In the situation room at Pacific Fleet headquarters MacArthur gave a map talk that was enormously impressive, and convinced Roosevelt that the drive back to the Philippines was essential for political and not military purposes. The President was not a great military strategist, perhaps, but he was a political genius, and MacArthur showed him that the recapture of the Philippines would redeem an American promise that had to have enormous effect on the people of Asia. Admiral Nimitz had no effective counterarguments to make, so the President went back to Washington convinced of the soundness of the MacArthur plan.

At the end of the conference, MacArthur was jubilant.

"We've sold it," he told an aide, as he boarded his plane to go back to Brisbane and the war.

And indeed, MacArthur had persuaded President Roosevelt to change the entire war plan. The leadership would go from Admiral Nimitz and the Pacific Fleet to General MacArthur and the Southwest Pacific command. The army would lead the drive to Tokyo, by way of Manila.

The change was not then irreversible. The President was convinced but the Joint Chiefs of Staff were not, and if they presented a united front against the MacArthur plan, the President would have gone along, particularly, as seemed likely, if the Combined Chiefs of Staff (British and American) had opted to show opposition to what Admiral King called the wasteful process of "battering our way through the Philippines."

Another factor, however, intervened that summer in favor of the change of operational leadership of the Pacific War from navy to army hands: When the Americans invaded Saipan, the whole show was the navy's. Admiral Spruance was in command of the overall invasion. Admiral Richmond Kelly Turner was in command of the amphibious force and the troops until the beachhead was declared to be secure. Then Marine Lieutenant General Howland Smith took command. But not all the troops ashore, by far, were Marines. The army's Twenty-seventh Division was also involved. And that was the rub.

The army's Twenty-seventh Division was a National Guard organization that had been brought almost intact to the Pacific in the early days of the war. It had participated in the invasion of the Gilberts and of the Marshall Islands. But General Howland Smith had never been happy with the division's operations. Privately the Marines said that the division was a mess of cronyism and corruption, and that the top officers were incompetent.

"Howling Mad" Smith had spoken very harshly to and about General Ralph Smith of the Twenty-seventh Division at the time of the Gilberts campaign, and again in the Marshalls. During the Saipan invasion, the Twenty-seventh Division had been held in reserve but had to be committed to action very soon because of the strenuous nature of the Japanese defense. And once it was committed, it did very little to help the American effort. The division bogged down, and it seemed that it could not be made to move. Finally, in exasperation, General Howland Smith relieved General Ralph Smith of command. The new commander, Major General Jarman, relieved some key officers as well, and the division began to move. But the scandal rocked Washington. It was unheard of for a Marine general to relieve an army general, and not acceptable, said the army and the army's friends in Congress.

And so, privately, the army generals indicated that they would never again serve under a Marine general, and all this got to President Roosevelt and to the Joint Chiefs of Staff, and had an effect on the outcome of the Pacific campaign. All the rest of that summer and into early fall, Admiral King fought the battle of Formosa v. the Philippines, but he was losing ground steadily because of the political climate that existed in Washington.

Meanwhile the planning for the invasion of the Palau Islands by the Pacific Fleet and of Halmahera by MacArthur's Navy continued.

At this same time the Japanese were also making some plans that would have a major effect on the operations in the Pacific War, beginning that autumn.

(*Left to right*) Rear Admiral Russell S. Berkey, General Douglas MacArthur, and Vice-Admiral Thomas Kinkaid confer aboard the USS *Phoenix* while enroute to Milne Bay during the invasion of the Admiralty Islands, February 27, 1944.

(*U.S. Army Signal Corps/MacArthur Memorial*)

General MacArthur views the body of a dead Japanese on the airstrip on Los Negros Island, just fifteen minutes after the enemy soldier was killed, February 2, 1944. Vice-Admiral Kinkaid stands behind MacArthur.　　(*U.S. Army Signal Corps/MacArthur Memorial*)

Douglas MacArthur aboard a U.S. Navy PT boat in April 1944.
(U.S. Army Signal Corps/MacArthur Memorial)

MacArthur and his staff with the troops at Tanahmerah Bay (Papua New Guinea), April 22, 1944. At the left, wearing a hat rather than a helmet, is Rear Admiral Daniel E. Barbey.
(U.S. Army Signal Corps/MacArthur Memorial)

General Douglas MacArthur and Admiral Chester W. Nimitz pose for photographers beside a map of the Pacific Ocean. *(U.S. Navy/MacArthur Memorial)*

Several staff officers at a conference of General MacArthur and Admiral Nimitz at Brisbane in March 1944: *(left to right)* Captain Cato D. Glover (ass't. plans officer, 7th Fleet), Major General Richard J. Marshall (deputy chief of staff, GHQ), Lieutenant General George Kenney (CG, 5th Air Force), Lieutenant General Richard K. Sutherland (chief of staff, SWPA), Vice-Admiral Thomas C. Kinkaid (commander, Allied Naval Forces SWPA), Rear Admiral Forrest P. Sherman (ass't. chief of staff, 7th Fleet), and Major General Stephan J. Chamberlin (G-3 officer, SWPA). *(U.S. Army Signal Corps/MacArthur Memorial)*

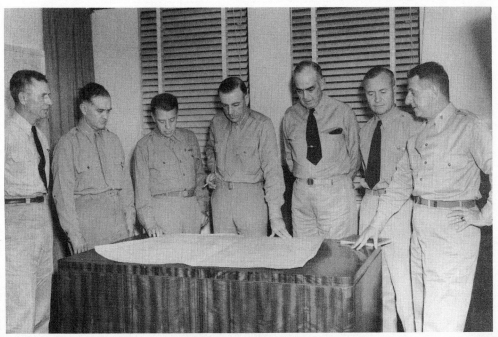

During the landings at Morotai Island in September 1944, an LCI(R) (landing craft, infantry, rocket) fires on the beaches during the first wave.
(U.S. Army Signal Corps/MacArthur Memorial)

Carrying troops of the 124th Infantry, an LVT-4 (landing vehicle, tracked, Mark 4), also known as an alligator, lands on Morotai Island on September 15, 1944.
(U.S. Army Signal Corps/MacArthur Memorial)

Troops of the 31st Infantry Division unload off an LCI (landing craft, infantry, large) at Morotai Island, September 15, 1944. *(U.S. Army Signal Corps/MacArthur Memorial)*

Members of the 2nd Battalion, 124th Infantry Regiment, wade in from LCIs (landing craft, infantry, large) to land on the beach at Morotai Island. Note the height of the water at the end of the gangplank as men step off the craft.

(U.S. Army Signal Corps/MacArthur Memorial)

A Japanese Betty bomber crashes close to an unidentified aircraft carrier in the Pacific.
(U.S. Navy/MacArthur Memorial)

A U.S. Navy TBF-1 Avenger crashes near an unidentified aircraft carrier somewhere in the Pacific. The crew is seen escaping and preparing to inflate their life rafts.
(U.S. Navy/MacArthur Memorial)

A variety of invasion vessels is evident in this photograph of one of the landing beaches on Leyte in the Philippines, October 1944. The ship is a U.S. Navy LSM (landing ship, medium) seen in company with LCV (landing craft, vehicle) and LCM (landing craft, medium).

(U.S. Army Signal Corps/MacArthur Memorial)

An M-4 Sherman medium tank unloading from a U.S. Navy LSM (landing ship, medium) on Leyte in October 1944.

(U.S. Army Signal Corps/ MacArthur Memorial)

Riding a landing barge into Leyte on October 20, 1944, General MacArthur fulfills his promise to return to the Philippines. Riding along with MacArthur's staff members is Sergio Osmena *(third from left)*, president of the Philippine Commonwealth.

(U.S. Army Signal Corps/MacArthur Memorial)

The U.S. Navy submarine USS *Tambor* sinks a small Japanese merchant ship in the Pacific in June 1945. The crew is preparing to pick up Japanese survivors.

(U.S. Navy/MacArthur Memorial)

In March 1944, Premier Tojo himself had ordered army air force studies of special suicide missions. The Imperial Headquarters also sanctioned something very close to them: *Tan* missions, or "sincerity loyalty" missions, in which pilots were assigned targets beyond the ability of their aircraft to strike and return to base. The justification was that somehow the pilots would land somewhere and find their way home. But it was not believed by anybody.

And on a local level at Rabaul and elsewhere, *jibaku*, or self-crashing of pilots to destroy an enemy, was becoming ever more common.

On July 7, after the disastrous Battle of the Philippine Sea, and three days before the American flag was raised over Saipan, the Japanese army leaders held a meeting at which they ordered the building of special planes designed for one-way missions. The navy already had a number of "suicide weapons" under development, including the *kaiten*, or human torpedo, and the *ohka*, or human bomb.

Also, enormous pressure was building within the navy air service, at the operational level, for some way to try to stop the American enemy. In mid-June Vice-Admiral Shigeru Fukudome, commander of the Second Naval Air Fleet, had visited the Tateyama Air Base in Chiba Prefecture. There one of Japan's "ace" fighter pilots had spoken to the admiral. The ace was Captain Motoharu Okamura, who was in charge of the base's fighter command, and whose squadron had earned the name "Okamura's Circus" in operations against the Americans. Admiral Fukudome was impressed enough to take the matter up with Admiral Shimada, the chief of the naval general staff, a few days later.

And, again on the operational level, more pressure was brought when Captain Okamura went to see Commander Minoru Genda, the planner of the Pearl Harbor attack, who was now an important official in the Munitions Ministry, and Admiral Takejiro Ohnishi, who had been Genda's superior in the planning. It just so happened that at the time of that meeting, Lieutenant General Saburo Endop of the army's aerial weapons bureau was visiting Ohnishi, so the Okamura plan for suicide weapons got a wider audience than he had anticipated.

That is how the pressure spread across Japan at every military level, spurred on by the growing sense of defeat within Japan, and the knowledge that defeat was unacceptable.

After the fall of Saipan, Admiral Ohnishi, who had become an enthusiast for suicide operations, tried to get to Emperor Hirohito through the emperor's brother, who was a naval officer and a friend of Ohnishi's, but he was blocked by palace officials.

After the fall of the Tojo cabinet in mid-July, Ohnishi took his case to the newspapers and gave the story of the suicide plan to *Yomiuri Shimbun,* one of Japan's three national newspapers.

On July 21 Admiral Shimada presented Admiral Toyoda, the Combined Fleet commander, with a new operational advisory, and it included the use of suicide planes. The next day Admiral Mitsumasa Yonai and General Kuniako Koiso were appointed to head the new government of Japan. Admiral Ohnishi called on Admiral Yonai that same evening at home and presented his plan. A few days later Ohnishi was appointed to command the First Naval Air Fleet in the Philippines.

On August 20, when American B-29s from Chengdu hit the Yawata Steelworks on Kyushu Island, one Japanese suicide pilot managed to climb high enough to crash a plane, and in a fluke he managed to hit two B-29s and bring them both down. This feat was a great convincer to the Japanese air-defense officials.

That summer both army and navy proceeded to build special suicide weapons. By early September the navy had produced two prototype flying bombs. By October the army and the navy had both organized special suicide commands.

And that summer the American Joint Chiefs of Staff continued to ponder the problems of the Pacific War. In the second week of September 1944, they went to Quebec, to meet the British chiefs of staff, President Franklin D. Roosevelt, and Prime Minister Winston Churchill to settle on the plan for the coming months. On September 15, they decided, General MacArthur's Navy would occupy Morotai, an island off Halmahera. This move was to be the first step toward Mindanao, in the Philippines, which General MacArthur was to attack by the end of the year. If enough ships could have been made available, General MacArthur would have gone straight to Mindanao, but in the summer of 1944 the invasion of Normandy had demanded an enormous effort, so MacArthur had to be content with a two-stage attack. Halmahera had been considered as the attack point, but it was very heavily defended by the Japanese, with nine airfields, and so nearby Morotai, which would serve the same purpose as a staging point for Mindanao, was substituted.

To capture Morotai, MacArthur chose the Eleventh Corps, under Major General Charles P. Hall. It was built around the Thirty-first Division, which had gotten some experience in mopping up operations in the Wakde-Sarmi area of New Guinea.

Admiral Kinkaid turned the Morotai operation over to Admiral Barbey, and he chose two beaches of landings. He would supervise landings on Beach White, and Admiral Fechteler would handle Beach Red. The immediate object was to capture the Pitoe airstrip, which the Japanese had built. The attacks would be covered by the cruiser group, now commanded by Rear Admiral R. S. Berkey, and by the escort carrier force of six carriers, commanded by Rear Admiral Thomas L. Sprague. So MacArthur's Navy did have its own carriers, although these were still totally underrated. More important to the naval planners was the loan of Task Group 38.1 under Vice-Admiral John S. McCain for a few days.

MacArthur's Navy was growing again. For the Morotai landing Rear Admiral Barbey would have his flagship, the *Wasatch* command ship, a pair of Australian attack transports, five destroyer transports, forty-five LSTs, twenty-four LCIs, twenty LCTs, and a landing ship dock, a clumsy-looking vessel that was immensely valuable because it provided a sort of pier facility. The attack force would be covered not only by the cruisers, but by its own screen of twenty-four destroyers, four frigates, eleven LCIs fitted out as rocket vessels, half a dozen patrol boats, four minesweepers, and a pair of tugs to be there in case any ship got into trouble. The attack force came from Hollandia and from Biak, and the ships assembled off the Vogelkop. It was September 13. Meanwhile, Admiral Halsey, who had taken over the Pacific Fleet striking force, had been besieging the southern Philippine Islands. After several days of such attack, on September 13 he and his staff talked about the lack of Japanese air opposition to the carrier fleet, and he sent a message to Admiral Nimitz suggesting that the whole timetable set up by the Joint Chiefs of Staff be shucked as unnecessary, and that the seizure of Leyte Island, which had now become the focus of the Joint Chiefs' planning, be moved up by several months. That would mean that the Morotai landings, and even those on Mindanao, were unnecessary.

But with the invasion force already at sea, it was too late to stop the process. So the Morotai landing went off as scheduled.

D-Day was September 15. This landing was considered by General MacArthur to be the first step on his way back to Manila. He came along, riding in the cruiser *Nashville*.

The initial proceedings were not very exciting. The *Nashville* and the other cruisers laid down their barrages. There was no reply from guns on the shore. The main convoy came up between Cape Gila and Mirita Island, the LSTs towing the LCTs, and then the LCTs were cast off and all ships formed a column for the passage in toward Morotai. They were led by the minesweepers, but no mines were discovered. And when the troops moved into the landing craft and sped ashore, there was no Japanese opposition. The real opposition was caused by nature. The aerial photographs of Morotai had not shown the composition of the beach that sloped up to it. The beach was mud. And consequently when the LCTs put their vehicles ashore in what seemed to be very shallow water, they got bogged down in the mud, and about three-quarters of them had to be pulled out by bulldozers.

On Beach White, Admiral Barbey's troops had to wade ashore through water as high as their shoulders. The LSTs grounded a hundred yards off the beach. Only later did the searchers find some better beaches for the landings. If the Japanese had been there in force, the results of the Morotai landing might have been nearly disastrous, but as it was, the word was "inconvenient."

It was not long after noon on D-Day that General Persons of the Thirty-first Division established his command post ashore. Not a shot had yet been fired by a Japanese. But that night some action developed, and the enemy staged some banzai charges that were promptly wiped out. The whole garrison of the island had numbered about five hundred, and most of them were killed, although about two hundred had managed to escape into the mountains. After the first day a few halfhearted air raids came in from Halmahera, but they did very little damage. The reason, not really perceived by the Americans, was that the Japanese were husbanding their air strength throughout the South Pacific for the coming "big battle," which they now expected to develop in the Philippines.

The Morotai operation was attended by one tragedy. On October 3 the fighting was really over, and the escort carriers were about to leave the island area. They were attacked by a Japanese submarine, and one of the screening destroyers was torpedoed and later sank. The carriers and destroyers then began a furious search for the submarine, and they found one, but unfortunately the submarine that they found, attacked, and sank with all hands, was the U.S.S. *Seawolf*, which was carrying passengers and supplies to the Philippine guerrillas in Mindanao. The *Seawolf* was traveling in a safety zone, and Admiral Kinkaid of MacArthur's Navy had issued warnings, but the men of the carriers and destroyers were too excited to take care.

By October 4, the island was secured. No attempt was made to go up into the mountains and track down the Japanese. That was unnecessary. The Allies had what they wanted: the Morotai airstrips, from which the Allies could stage fighter planes and medium bombers up to Leyte bases when the time came.

And the time was very near.

13

THE LEYTE PLAN

The Joint Chiefs of Staff's change of direction and the decision to invade the Philippines instead of Formosa brought a major change to the conduct of the Pacific War. General MacArthur really was in charge now of the route back to Japan, and the Pacific Fleet stepped back to take a supporting role.

In fact, this change reestablished the order of command as it always should have been; the role of the navy in the first two and a half years of the Pacific War really created an anomaly in the command function. It worked only because of the existence of that one organization the Joint Chiefs of Staff, which made an attempt at really unified planning, although there was no unification of the military services.

The control of the Joint Chiefs of Staff kept the American war effort from deteriorating as did the Japanese. For even though Japan was *in extremis* in the summer of 1944, the Japanese army and navy still found it impossible to really combine efforts. Nowhere was this more apparent than in the air. The army received half the output of Japan's aircraft factories each month, although the navy was responsible for air defense of the island empire, and the army planes supported only army operations. Even a few weeks before the next American move, when the Japanese had a very good idea that the Philippines would be attacked, the army had many aircraft available in the islands, but the navy, worn down by attrition, had very few. All around the southern defense perimeter, the navy was stretched to the breaking point, while the army basked in comparative luxury of equipment. Until the fall of the Tojo government the army had been running the Imperial General Headquarters, itself an army creation presented by Tojo to maintain army control of the war effort. Only after the Imperial Navy was taken in as a full partner in the establishment of the joint government of General Koiso and Admiral Yonai did it begin to have a part in the general defense planning of Japan. By that time the Combined Fleet had been so decimated by Allied air and sea power that it was no longer worthy of the name. The navy had just about enough strength left for one great last gasp, and this was proposed to happen in the Philippines, with much exterior gusto and confidence, and the private pessimism of almost all the admirals. A few days after the creation of the new government, Admiral Toyoda, new commander in chief of the Combined Fleet, called on Admiral Yonai in Yonai's capacity as Navy Minister.

"Can we hold out until the end of the year?" the minister asked the commander.

"It will probably be extremely difficult to do so," said Admiral Toyoda.

It was not that the Japanese did not understand what was happening. Indeed Japanese strategic understanding throughout the Pacific War surpassed that of the Americans. In August, after the fall of Saipan, the Japanese knew that the next American moves would be to the Philippines and the Ryukyu Islands. How did the Japanese know? Because it was the logical next step, although it took the American Joint Chiefs of Staff another two months to agree on it. In the Japanese basic defense plan only one proviso indicated the outside chance that the next American move might be toward Formosa, rather than the Philippines, but almost all bets were that the Americans would take the road to Manila, and that is why in the summer of 1944, the pugnacious Admiral Ohnishi was chosen to head the naval air defense of the Philippines.

As of early October there really was no further question in the Japanese mind. The capture of Morotai was made at the same time as the Pacific Fleet's invasion of the Palau Islands, where the Combined Fleet had been headquartered for a short time. The fight was attenuated, because the Japanese had learned a great deal about defense in the Southwest Pacific campaign. At Buna the Japanese had put up an extremely powerful defense, with relatively few resources, and at Biak they had delayed the Allies for weeks by doing the same. Even the generals understood the nature of the new war they faced: Japan had lost the initiative, and all the rest of this war was going to be a matter of holding out to the death, and trying to make the cost of victory so high for the Allies that they would give up their demands for unconditional surrender, and offer Japan a negotiated peace that would save pride if not much of the rest of the empire. That is what the war was about, from the Japanese point of view, as of September 1944.

Admiral Ohnishi was preparing to leave for the Philippines. The army was sending General Tomoyuki Yamashita, "the tiger of Malaya," who had defeated the British at Singapore. The key to the defense against the landings that would be made by MacArthur's Navy was the air forces. The Japanese Fifth Base Air Force was commanded by Vice-Admiral K. Teraoka. In September it had about six hundred planes. The army's Fourth Air Army had a few less. Also the defense would be aided by planes from Kyushu and Formosa, where the Sixth Base Air Force operated, and that force had about eight hundred fifty aircraft, including a highly vaunted unit; the T Force (T for "typhoon" to recall the Great Typhoon that had devastated the Chinese attackers in the thirteenth century and that became the prototype for the Kamikaze pilots).

For months the Japanese had been saying that although their carrier air force had been hard hit, they really did not need it anymore because the war had changed so that the island empire itself offered all sorts of air bases. It was true: There were eleven naval air stations on Formosa, fifteen army airfields, and two seaplane bases; ten air bases on Luzon Island, eight on Leyte, and twenty more on the Visaya islands of Negros, Cebu, and Mindanao. The rub was that the permanent airfield could not maneuver to escape attack.

As the Allies planned for their landings in Leyte, the Japanese surface fleet also planned for its counterattack. The major elements of the fleet were located at Lingga Roads, near Singapore, to remain close to the fuel supply. The carrier forces had gone back to Japan to the Inland Sea, seeking safety for training operations.

And at Tokyo the Imperial General Staff planned for Operation Sho (*sho*: victory). It was hailed as a mighty combined effort of naval air force, army air force, navy and army, to stop the Allies in their tracks and turn the war around.

And of all this the Allies were blissfully unaware. General MacArthur, in particular, did not believe that the Allies would have much more trouble in the Philippines than they had had at Morotai. His intelligence estimates indicated that the Japanese were continually drawing back and weakening, and that is what the headquarters anticipated as the course of events in October and November 1944. Everything seemed to point to an easy victory; one intelligence estimate said that it would be impractical for the Japanese to make a defensive approach to Leyte through Surigao Strait. These intelligence bulletins were not only useless, they were dead wrong, as it would turn out.

To stage the invasion of the Philippines, General MacArthur was given the greatest force yet assembled in the Pacific. The reason, of course, was that the invasion of Europe had been accomplished, and after some worrisome days the Normandy beachhead had been secured, the port of Cherbourg had been taken, and the Allies had broken out of Normandy and seemed to be moving rapidly on the conquest of Hitler Europe. More matériel, therefore, was readily available for the Pacific.

MacArthur would command the ground forces, the air forces, and the Seventh Fleet, and he would be supported by Admiral Nimitz's Pacific Fleet striking force, called the Third Fleet, since it was operating under Admiral Halsey. In this sense "supported by" would become a very important term because of a controversy that would develop between Halsey and Admiral Kinkaid, but in brief, "supported by" meant that Admiral Halsey would do all possible to assist the operations of MacArthur's Navy, but that he was not bound by their wishes and they had no control over him.

Indeed, Admiral Halsey's orders from Nimitz said that he would first strike Okinawa, Formosa, and northern Leyte, and then hit the southern Philippines to support the actual landings on Leyte, between October 16 and October 20, and then he would operate in support of the Leyte landings by destroying Japanese naval and air forces that threatened the landings.

"In case opportunity for destruction of major portions of the enemy fleet is offered or can be created, such destruction becomes the primary task," said the orders.

And that seemed quite proper, for Admiral Kinkaid's Seventh Fleet was a mighty power in itself. It was so large for this attack that Admiral Kinkaid had two subordinate commanders, a Northern Attack Force under Rear Admiral Barbey and a Southern Attack Force under Rear Admiral Theodore S. Wilkinson. Barbey had more than twenty-five

2823

attack transports and cargo ships. There was no more shoestring for Admiral Barbey, no more commanding of a landing from a destroyer; for this operation he had the *Blue Ridge,* a modern communications ship, as his flagship.

Admiral Wilkinson's command was almost a duplicate. His flagship was the special amphibious command ship *Mount Olympus;* his command was also split in two, and each of his subordinate commanders, Rear Admiral R. L. Conolly and Rear Admiral F. B. Royal, had his own command ship.

Then, after the landings, there would come up three separate groups of reinforcing ships, scores and scores of vessels. Reinforcement Group Number Two, for example, under Captain J. K. B. Ginder, included thirty-three LSTs, twenty-four Liberty ships and other merchant ships, and a dozen naval service ships.

Surrounding all these payload ships were cruisers and destroyers—scores of destroyers—and two fleet units that had to be considered major units in anyone's language. One was Fire Support Unit North, under Rear Admiral G. L. Weyler. It included the battleships *Mississippi, Maryland,* and *West Virginia,* three light cruisers (under separate command), and half a dozen destroyers. The other command was Fire Support Unit South, under Rear Admiral J. B. Oldendorf. It was made up of the battleships *Tennessee, California,* and *Pennsylvania,* five cruisers, a dozen destroyers, and all sorts of tugs, repair ships, and other service ships. Also under separate command was a group of four Australian and American cruisers, and seven destroyers.

And besides all that sea power, a whole escort carrier group came along to protect the landings. It consisted of three smaller units called "Taffies," totaling 18 small carriers, each mounting 25 to 35 planes, or an air armada of 503 aircraft, which was just 80 planes fewer than had been carried by the Pacific Fleet's entire carrier task force at the time of the invasion of the Marshall Islands a few months earlier. Once again, Rear Admiral Thomas Sprague's escort carrier group was the most highly underrated force in the entire American navy.

This great armada began to assemble. The task of the Third Fleet was to strike the air bases of the southern Philippines in September and then move on to Formosa, and this was done. Most of the Japanese naval and army air forces were destroyed in this series of attacks. And then on October 10 began the extensive air battle of Formosa, in which Halsey's fleet raised havoc with the Japanese defenses of Formosa and southern Kyushu, and stopped their drive down to the Philippines.

Meanwhile, early in October, the elements of the Seventh Fleet and the troops it would deliver to Leyte were beginning to concentrate at Manus and along the coast of New Guinea. MacArthur's Navy was truly an armada, more than seven hundred ships, a more powerful force than the Allies had used in June to assault the European continent at Normandy.

14

LEYTE: BEGINNINGS

For many months the Japanese had puzzled over the tactics that they would use to oppose the Allies in the "ultimate battle" they sought, the naval battle that they hoped would even the sides and make possible a negotiated peace.

The Imperial General Headquarters knew of the immense power of the American navy by 1944, although even to them the reality was staggering. After the Battle of the Philippine Sea, in which they had lost the basic units of their carrier force, they had to regard their carriers in a new way, and they decided that they would be used as bait, to draw the American fleet away from the scene of the final battle, while the Japanese surface fleet, still mounting the most powerful battleships in the world, would take on the American landing forces and "annihilate" them.

Particularly, the Japanese intended to use the two carriers *Ise* and *Hyuga* for this purpose. These were hermaphrodite ships—they had been designed and built as surface warships, but in the need for carriers, they had been converted, some of their guns had been removed, and flight decks had been added to the ships. Now they were to be part of the Main Force, as the Japanese called it, in the great naval battle to come.

This group of ships, commanded by Vice-Admiral Jisaburo Ozawa, included the last great carrier of the Japanese fleet, the *Zuikaku,* whose sister ship, the *Shokaku,* had been sunk in the Battle of the Philippine Sea. The other carriers involved were the *Zuiho, Chitose,* and *Chiyoda,* all light carriers, and two of them were converted seaplane carriers at that. Besides that, in the Main Force there were three light cruisers and nine destroyers, plus oilers and six destroyer escorts. This force was to be used to lure the American carrier fleet away from the point of attack so the Japanese battleships could wreck the invasion.

The wreckage was to be created by most of what was left of the Imperial Japanese Navy, and this was not an inconsiderable body of ships.

First was what came to be called the Center Striking Force, under Vice-Admiral T. Kurita. It was built around battleship Division One, under Vice-Admiral Matome Ugaki. That division was further built around two ships, the *Yamato* and the *Musashi,* prides of the prewar Japanese fleet and the world's most powerful ships, each displacing 68,000 tons and armed with 9 eighteen-inch guns, plus a staggering number of smaller guns, and 125 antiaircraft guns. Each of these ships could travel at seventeen knots. With them traveled Cruiser Division Four, which consisted of four heavy cruisers, and Cruiser Division Five, another two cruisers, plus a light cruiser and nine destroyers.

Also traveling with this fleet, and part of the major striking force intended for the landing beaches, was a section of ships under the command of Vice-Admiral Yoshio Suzuki. This consisted of the older battleships *Kongo* and *Haruna,* four cruisers, one light cruiser, and six destroyers.

While the Main Force was to decoy the Americans and the Center Force hit the beaches from some point, two more striking forces would attack from another point, to complete the plan.

One of these units was the Southern Force, led by Vice-Admiral Shoji Nishimura, and it consisted of the battleships *Yamashiro* and *Fuso,* the heavy cruiser *Mogami,* and four destroyers.

The final group of ships to be employed by the Japanese was called the Second Striking Force. Its commander was Vice-Admiral Kiyohide Shima. It had no battleships but did include the heavy cruisers *Nachi* and *Ashigara,* the light cruiser *Abukuma,* and seven destroyers. Once the Japanese naval elements had hit the Leyte beaches and smashed the American invasion, the cap would be put on the victory by Vice-Admiral Naomasa Sakonju, who would bring a large army reinforcing unit to Leyte to mop up the beaches where the American troops would have been stranded by the destruction of the American invasion fleet. This naval force was made up of the heavy cruiser *Aoba,* the light cruiser *Kinu,* and six destroyers. They would carry troops from Mindanao to the far side of Leyte and land them to augment the Thirty-fifth Army, which was entrusted with the defense of Leyte.

The Japanese plan also called for the massive support of naval and army air units, and as of early September, when the plan was conceived, this element seemed very strong. Admiral Ohnishi was coming to put his considerable skill to directing the air defenses, and he had the new idea of organizing suicide units, to make the best use of the planes available. One Kamikaze, one carrier, was the dream. With perhaps a thousand army and navy planes in the Philippines, a large reserve back on Formosa and Kyushu, and a promise from the naval air high command that it could supply a thousand planes if necessary, along with the army's ability to supply its half of production—about fifteen hundred planes per month—the future seemed bright enough.

So the Japanese prepared for what they knew had to be the last great naval battle in the defense of the homeland. If this desperate gambit failed . . .

In September the Japanese prepared on land and sea for a battle in the Philippines. Admiral Toyoda made a trip to

Manila to see for himself how the land lay. Army inspection teams came down, and they discovered that General Shigenori Kuroda, the commander of the Philippine defenses, had become corrupted by the soft life of a garrison commander. He was replaced by General Yamashita, the conqueror of Malaya, who came down in September to organize the defense. General Yamashita swiftly discovered two negative factors that would militate in favor of the Americans. First was Yamashita's realization that the Japanese occupation policy had been so far wrong that the "Republic of the Philippines," established as a puppet state within the Greater East Asia Coprosperity Sphere, was a sham, and that the hearts of the Filipino people either had remained with the Americans or had turned back to them. This matter would be very important in the months to come, from the first day that an American pilot would parachute down to safety in the jungle or on the beach and would then be kept and protected by the Filipinos, to the end when villagers would report to the Americans on the whereabouts of scattered Japanese troop units.

The second negative factor Yamashita discovered was that General Kuroda had been so corrupt and so careless that the Philippines' defense forces had no more than a few weeks' supply of food and matériel to conduct a defense. At Rabaul there were thousands of tons of supplies in warehouses and caves, stacked up by a careful army command. In Manila and elsewhere in the islands there was virtually nothing. The news was so electrifying that it prompted General Yamashita to the gloomy observation that this was a hopeless task.

The general's morale was not raised in September when the marauding Third Fleet under Admiral Halsey cut deeply into the air defense capabilities of the Japanese forces. Day after day Halsey's planes raided the airfields of Mindanao, Negros, Cebu, and the rest of the southern Philippines. Not content with that, they hit Manila and Clark Field's big complex of satellite fields. General Yamashita learned then the error of the army system of sending pilots to air units in the field without adequate training. The system had been invented in the Guadalcanal days to speed up the reinforcement of air units. A pilot would be trained to fly, although there was no time to instruct him properly in aerial navigation. Then he would be sent to an air unit, where the experienced pilots were expected to teach him how to engage in aerial combat with the enemy and to support the troops. The result of this system, General Yamashita learned, was the loss of many half-trained pilots in those September days, when they came up to challenge the very skillful American pilots of the carrier air squadrons.

After the Third Fleet raids on the Visayas and the rest of the Philippines, by the beginning of October the Philippine air defenses were in shambles. The army was extremely loath to release its loss figures, even to the Imperial Navy, but when Admiral Fukudome counted up, he found that he had fewer than two hundred navy planes instead of the thousand that he had expected. And the Battle of Formosa had precisely the effect on the coming Sho Operation that Admirals Nimitz, Halsey, and Kinkaid had wanted; Admiral Toyoda could not have the support of thousands of aircraft; too many had been destroyed. Once again, the army and navy systems militated against the Japanese in the moment of crisis. Several thousand aircraft were available in Japan. Sometimes half of them made it all the way. Sometimes 80 percent of a unit might make it. The losses were truly staggering, running more than 20 percent.

Admiral Ohnishi, as noted, considered his options. As an air admiral he had a fine regard for carriers, but there were no more. What he did expect were a large number of planes, and he was well aware (since he had a part in the planning) of the desultory nature of the Japanese naval air training program. So what he considered, prompted by many junior officers, was a program of making the best use of the air resources and human resources at hand in

Japan's critical hour. The Kamikaze concept was growing stronger in his mind all the time, and he had by this time realized that the same was true within the army, although the high command did not like to talk about it; and at the operational level such admirals as Fukudome were horrified by this waste of human life.

Communications between Tokyo and Manila were not so good that September of 1944 that Admiral Ohnishi had a very clear idea of what was happening in the Philippines. The American Third Fleet ranged around the islands, blasting Japanese installations and knocking down ever more aircraft.

Ohnishi was in Tokyo on October 1, when the navy acceded to the establishment of the 721st Naval Air Corps, a new organization dedicated to the development and operation of the *ohka*, or flying bomb. It would be delivered to a target by a twin-engined bomber that would release the piloted bomb a few thousand yards from its destination. The idea was all very well, said Admiral Ohnishi, but it was months away from fruition, and the Sho Plan was going to have to be implemented in a matter of weeks, from all he could see around him. The American attacks on the Philippines' air bases certainly presaged a land invasion soon.

And so Admiral Ohnishi called on the chief of the naval general staff, Admiral Oikawa, on the eve of Ohnishi's departure for Manila and sought official approval for beginning the Kamikaze program immediately in the Philippines.

Admiral Oikawa did not like the idea at all. He would have liked to veto it. But Ohnishi's arguments were very compelling, and they were not the first that Oikawa had heard: Given the state of Japan's naval air force, the suicide attacks made a great deal of sense, he said. But one thing must be made clear: The program was voluntary, and no man need go unless he wanted to. In their meeting on October 5, Admiral Ohnishi agreed to this stricture, and they parted with the understanding that Ohnishi would try the plan. Ohnishi then called on Commander Genda, the attack plan specialist, and they talked about establishing a new organization, which would be called the Kamikaze Special Attack Corps, but it would not be officially organized or recognized until Ohnishi had tried it out in the Philippines.

Admiral Ohnishi then left Tokyo for Manila on October 9, to take over the First Naval Air Fleet. He flew down to Kanoya air base in Kyushu, the first stop on the way to Manila. And while he was there, the American Third Fleet began its operations against Okinawa and Formosa, which would be known as the Great Formosa Air Battle. In order to get to Manila, Ohnishi had to detour to Shanghai and then fly to Taiwan.

And so Admiral Ohnishi came to Manila on October 17. He called on Vice-Admiral Shigeru Fukudome, commander of the Second Naval Air Fleet, and they assessed the naval air situation following the rounds of American attacks. Ohnishi's new command, he learned, did not number around a thousand aircraft. After those attacks, only forty planes (estimated) were operational. The disaster was numbing, but something had to be done. Admiral Ohnishi mentioned the idea of the Kamikazes. Admiral Fukudome did not like it. Several of his own pilots had suggested the same, but the admiral had refused to listen to them. The admirals did agree that something had to be done. That day they combined the First and Second Air Fleets, and as senior officer, Admiral Fukudome became commander, and Admiral Ohnishi stepped down to second place. The combined air fleet numbered around three hundred planes. Ohnishi said no more to Fukudome. After the three-day lambasting by Admiral Halsey, the air force at Taiwan was down to about three hundred planes. More planes were available in Japan, but they had to be flown to Kyushu, then to the Ryukyus, to Taiwan, and across the island chain to Clark Field.

On the morning of October 19, Admiral Ohnishi drove to Mabalacat airfield north of Manila, to talk over the problems of the naval air force. Captain Sakae Yamamoto was commander of Ohnishi's most effective operational unit at the moment, the 201st Air Group. Ohnishi decided that this group would become the nucleus of the Kamikaze Corps. Within twenty-four hours he had twenty-three volunteers, all eager to give their lives for the Emperor in this glorious cause.

"You are already gods," Admiral Ohnishi told the assembled young men, and he promised that he, personally, would report on the death of each of them to the Emperor. In such heady rhetoric was born the greatest threat yet aimed at Admiral Kinkaid and MacArthur's Navy.

15

LANDINGS ON LEYTE

For some unlucky dogfaces, the invasion of Leyte started on October 4. That was the day several units of Major General F. C. Sibert's Tenth Corps were loaded into LSTs in New Guinea and started for the invasion, nearly two thousand miles away at Leyte Gulf. For the next sixteen days they would be buffeted about at sea before they hit the beach.

It was very tough scheduling, but Admiral Barbey, the commander of the Seventh Fleet Amphibious Force, was used to it. He had supervised fourteen assault landings on various beaches and islands in the past year, and he was ready for almost anything.

Other units of Tenth Corps were luckier. Some of them managed to make a rehearsal of the landings, which gave them some experience in getting out of ships and into boats. Major General John R. Hodge's Twenty-fourth Corps was lucky enough to have as its rehearsal grounds the Hawaiian island of Maui, where the men were put ashore by Rear Admiral T. S. Wilkinson's Third Amphibious command. And some of the Tenth Corps men also got a rehearsal. Then the ships of the invasion, some 700 strong, began congregating at Seeadler Harbor and in Humboldt Bay, making ready for the big day.

111

On October 10, the day that Admiral Halsey's ships and planes began raising hob with the Japanese in the Ryukyus and on Formosa, ships began moving out toward Leyte Gulf. The rendezvous point for the invasion fleet would be a dot on the chart off the entrance to Leyte Gulf. The first ships were expected to arrive there on October 17.

The first ships to arrive in the area were minesweepers and survey ships. The former would assure the safety of the coastal area, the latter would augment the information on the old charts that were used by the invading forces. They left Manus on October 10, and promptly ran into a storm, for this was typhoon season in Philippine waters. The storm lasted for days and caused considerable damage to the ships. On October 16 they were straggling, and the speed of the force had to be cut to nine knots.

The approach of the minesweepers was aimed at Dinagat Island and three other islands at the edge of the Philippine Sea, which split the entrance to Leyte Gulf into two parts. The islands were manned by the Japanese. On Suluan Island the Japanese garrison occupied the tower of a lighthouse, an excellent observation point for watching the entrances to the gulf. Admiral Kinkaid had been cognizant of this Japanese lookout station, and eight destroyers had been allocated for the job of cleaning up there. They carried some five hundred troops of the American army's Sixth Ranger Battalion. The job of the troops would be to neutralize the islands.

The Dinagat Attack Group, as the naval force was called, reached Suluan at about six-thirty on the morning of October 17. A few minutes later the Japanese garrison in the lighthouse on Suluan sighted the American ships and radioed the word to Manila. They saw warships and carriers, and so stated. The carriers were there all right, but they were not the fleet carriers of Admiral Halsey, as the Japanese had assumed, but the large force of escort carriers under Rear Admiral Thomas L. Sprague that had been assigned to the Seventh Fleet. Within the hour Admiral

Toyoda knew that the major invasion, about which he was still not dead sure, would occur in the Philippines, and he acted accordingly. All the stops were removed. The Sho Plan was put into operation, and the ships of the various Japanese striking forces were ordered to sail.

An hour and a half after the sighting, the American ships moved into position to quiet the garrisons of the islands. There was no further question of surprise, but Admiral Kinkaid had not counted on it in this invasion. The number of ships was too large, and the logistical plans too diverse for surprise to be an effective factor. What was important was methodical clearance of the entryways and elimination of all obstacles. So the cruiser *Denver* opened up with her guns, to support the landing of the Rangers from the destroyer transports. One of the cruiser's first shells smashed the light in the lighthouse on Suluan, and the Japanese manning the light then scurried down and out into the brush. They ran into Filipinos who had been waiting for the day, and who directed the Rangers to the Japanese hiding places. Soon the Suluan garrison was finished, and the Rangers moved on. They had killed some thirty Japanese, with three casualties of their own.

The weather roughed up that day, and the next scheduled landing on Dinagat Island had to be delayed. But it really made no difference that they did not land until October 18, because the landing Rangers found that there were no Japanese left on the island. With the news from Suluan, they had evacuated to the Leyte hills. Or, some of them had. Others had been killed by Filipino guerrillas, who had been lying quiet for a long time, just waiting for this American invasion. The guerrillas turned over to the Rangers maps and other information about Japanese forces in the Leyte area.

More ships were coming up. The carriers and Admiral Oldendorf's battleships and cruisers that were going to bombard the Leyte beaches and prepare for the landings were waiting at the edge of the gulf.

The next step was the capture of Homonhon Island, where once more, no Japanese were found. So by noon on October 18, the entrances to Leyte Gulf were clear, the channel was being swept, and the expected Japanese gun positions found to be mythical.

Sweeping the channel proved to be difficult because of the high wind and seas. There were mines; the Japanese had laid a minefield between Dinagat and Homonhon islands, but these were mostly picked up and destroyed. Still some "floaters" remained.

Extreme caution would have demanded that the warships remain outside the channels until total safety could be guaranteed, but Admiral Oldendorf had to make a crucial decision: If he delayed the movement, the whole invasion would be set back a day, and he knew that Admiral Kinkaid would not appreciate that problem.

The next step called for Admiral Oldendorf's force to close on the waters off Dulag and send underwater demolition teams into the beaches to see what they could find. At noon on October 18 Oldendorf's ships were moving into this area, and two hours later the battleships and cruisers were prepared to bombard the landing coast.

The first bombardment of Leyte proper then began at 2 P.M. on October 18. The battleship *Pennsylvania* and the cruisers *Minneapolis* and *Denver* fired on assigned areas of the beach. The underwater demolition teams moved off from the destroyers, and it was then that the Americans discovered the Japanese on Leyte. The defenders watched the landing craft filled with underwater men as they came in, and when they were within range, they began firing with 75-mm guns, machine guns, and mortars. The destroyer *Goldsborough* came in to a point about a mile from the beach and began firing her four-inch guns. The Japanese's positions in the jungle were completely concealed, and no one aboard the ships had the impression that they were hitting anything. That negative impression was increased when one landing craft was sunk, and a shell struck the forward smokestack of the *Goldsborough* and killed two men. After a while the underwater teams came back after checking the beaches and reported that there were no obstacles to the landing.

So everything was ready for the landings, it seemed, and that night Admiral Oldendorf brought his force of fire support warships inside Leyte Gulf.

The next day, October 19, Admiral Oldendorf's bombardment group was to continue the softening up of the Leyte beaches, but that night of October 18 the destroyer *Ross,* moving along Homonhon Island, struck one of those floating mines, and then hit a second mine and was really in trouble. She was picked up by the tug *Chickasaw* and towed into an anchorage, where she was safe enough, but of no further use in the Battle of Leyte Gulf.

On the morning of October 19, Admiral Oldendorf's ships began shelling again, and Admiral Weyler's Northern Attack Force bombardment group also moved up to position to fire on Tacloban on the northwestern side of Leyte Gulf. The underwater demolition teams here also discovered good landing beaches, and no obstacles. The bombardment force began firing and was fired upon, and the destroyer *Aulick* was hit three times by shells from shore guns, without suffering major damage.

Offshore, the aircraft carriers of Admiral Sprague's escort group put their planes into the air that morning of October 19. Twelve of the carriers were off Leyte; the other six were escorting ships up from Manus and New Guinea for the landings.

It was a matter of some concern at General MacArthur's headquarters that day when Admiral Halsey announced that he was keeping his ships up north around Luzon Island, attacking northern airfields so that they could not transship planes south. The main reason for this decision was Halsey's hope that by staying put he would show himself as "bait" for the Japanese navy, and that the major fleet elements would come out to do battle. This decision marked a change; it had been assumed that Halsey would support the landings directly, although probably that had never been assumed by Halsey himself, since it was, in the carrier fleet's eyes, a job to be done by the escort carriers all the way through. Anyhow that is how it was on the nineteenth and would be, pretty much thereafter: Halsey was looking for major elements of the Japanese fleet to appear, and he felt that the escort carriers could quite well support the landings by themselves.

The planes of Admiral Sprague's escort carriers performed like veterans. They started early on the morning of October 19, hitting the Japanese defense installations and any ships or barges that moved in Leyte Gulf. They went back to the airfields of Cebu, Negros, Panay, and Mindanao, which had been thoroughly worked over in September by Admiral Halsey's planes, and they found some more aircraft, mostly on the ground. They destroyed a large number of them, against virtually no air opposition.

The pilots wondered why it was that the Japanese did not come out and fight. The reason was simpler than they might have thought: The Japanese air force had been ordered to hold all its strength until the Sho Plan was in force, and that meant five more days, October 24, when the Japanese ships would descend on the Leyte beaches in force and try to wipe out the Americans. Then the Japanese air force was supposed to act and strike the finishing blows.

The day was spent most constructively from the U.S. naval air force's point of view. By nightfall, the bombardment had been severe, most of the planes seen on the fields at the airstrips around Leyte had been knocked out, very little had been seen of the Japanese on the ground, and nothing of the Japanese ships at sea. Everything was going according to plan. The invasion fleet was on its way and at 11 P.M. on October 19 reached the assembly point off Dinagat Island. The men in the ships were waiting for dawn, and after that for 10 A.M. on October 20, for that is the time when the tides would be right and the landings were to begin. Admiral Barbey was heading for San Pedro Bay, and Admiral Wilkinson for Dulag.

At two o'clock on the morning of October 20, the American forces were getting into action for the landings on Leyte. The Northern Attack Force under Admiral Barbey moved into action: Rear Admiral A. D. Struble's ships headed off by themselves toward Panaon Island, off the southern point of Leyte; while Admiral Barbey led the other two groups of the Northern Attack Force, which then split in two, one unit to land on Beach White and the other on Beach Red, both near Tacloban. At 8 A.M. the transports were moving into position and the boats were put over the side. The men got down into them, and the coxswains began milling about, preparing to line up and move in to the beaches. Behind the landing forces, the bombardment group sent shells hurtling in at the Japanese, and in the morning light the planes of Admiral McCain's task group came whistling in to help after all, sweeping again over all those airfields in the southern Philippines. The escort carriers now kept the combat air patrol over the invasion forces, sixteen fighters and half a dozen torpedo bombers, ready for anything that might come along.

The air strikes and bombardment ended at 9:30 that morning, and the landing craft turned in circles, lined up, and swept in toward the beach.

First came the LCI rocket boats, firing their "swishers" when they reached a point three-quarters of a mile from the beach. They shot more than five thousand rockets onto Red and White beaches that morning. From the jungles the Japanese returned the fire, and the troops came in under shooting from guns in the hills and from automatic weapons along the shore.

The landings went very smoothly, until almost the last. Then the Japanese seemed to get the idea and the range, and in short order they hit three landing craft, sinking one of them and killing several men.

The Japanese also had good luck with the LSTs, which could not come in close enough to shore to discharge their vehicles. They were under fire, off Beach Red, and three of them were badly hit.

The LSTs had to wait offshore, under mortar fire, until pontoon units could be brought up to let them land their vehicles. But by noon, the landings were in good order, and after lunch General MacArthur, who had come up in the cruiser *Nashville* to watch the landings, made his symbolic trip ashore.

"Well," he said, smiling to his chief of staff, "believe it or not, we're here." He came ashore in a landing craft, and when it grounded in knee-deep water, he walked ashore soaking wet below the knees, and inspected the beach.

Then MacArthur made his famous speech on landing, addressed to the people of the Philippines.

"I have returned," he said.

And a few hours later, around the world, those words were in the headlines, and as President Roosevelt had known all along, they created an enormous sensation. The first major promise of the Pacific War had been redeemed by General MacArthur and by MacArthur's Navy.

16

REACTION

At ten o'clock on the morning of October 20, as the men of MacArthur's Navy were moving their ships into the shores of Leyte, the nucleus of Admiral Ohnishi's new Kamikaze air force prepared for action at Mabalacat, the air base north of Manila. Lieutenant Yukio Seki, a graduate of the Japanese naval academy at Eta-jima, was in command. He and twenty-three pilots lined up in the courtyard of the air base headquarters. Admiral Ohnishi soon came out and made a little speech.

The war was going very badly, the admiral told the men, so badly that only heroic measures could possibly turn the course of events. These young men would have to do what the Imperial Navy had so far failed to do: stop the American drive to Tokyo. The admiral spoke with deep emotion, then shook hands with each of the young pilots, got into his car, and was driven back to his headquarters. The new weapon had been forged. Vice-Admiral Teraoka, who did not believe in suicide tactics, was removed from his new command of the combined air fleets and sent back to Japan to a training command.

That day the first Kamikaze unit, called Yamato (the historic name for Japan), flew down to Cebu Island to prepare for the first attack.

The Americans were somewhat puzzled on the day of the landings, because no Japanese air force plane appeared to contest the landings. They moved ashore rapidly and inland, securing the beaches and driving the Japanese ahead of them. But by evening the skies were no longer empty of enemy aircraft. A single plane appeared at dusk and put a torpedo into the cruiser *Honolulu*, offshore with the Southern Landing Force, killing sixty men and putting the cruiser out of action.

On October 21 the Yamato Kamikaze unit took off from the Cebu airfield and headed for Leyte Gulf, but the weather that day was overcast and stormy, and the planes failed to find the American ships, so they returned to base. So, also, did the planes of the three other Kamikaze units from Mabalacat. But an army plane (for the army had rushed its own suicide units to the Philippines on the announcement of the Sho Operation) crashed into the Australian cruiser *Australia*, killing the captain and nineteen men, and injuring Commodore John Collins and fifty-three other men. The event did not seem particularly notable. There had been occasions before when Japanese pilots, their planes damaged beyond ability to return to base, had chosen to dive to death. So no particular notice was taken of the damage to the *Australia*, and she and the *Honolulu* were escorted back to Manus for repairs.

That second day the escort carriers were hard at work supporting the troops ashore with bombing and strafing raids, and attacking the Japanese airfields at Cebu, Negros, and the other islands near Leyte.

Admiral Kurita's First Striking Force had sailed away from Lingga Roads on October 18, bound for the Philippines by way of Brunei Bay in Borneo, where it refueled and then headed east. On October 20 Admiral Ozawa's group of carriers and cruisers also sailed from the Inland Sea. Altogether the carriers had only 116 planes aboard, and the *Ise* and the *Hyuga* had none at all. By October 22, all the Japanese naval units consigned to the attack were on their way. Admiral Shima was ordered to move out of Japan's Inland Sea and head for the Philippines, and Kurita's force was in the Palawan Passage and heading for the San Bernardino Strait, north of Leyte Island.

Off the beaches, the American ships of MacArthur's Navy waited for the Japanese to react to the landings. But except for the odd plane attacking, there seemed to be no reaction, so on October 21 the ships of the fast carrier force fueled and then headed to Ulithi for provisions and ammunition. Two groups of carriers stood by the Leyte area just in case.

On the ground, the American troops moved inland, and by the end of October 21 they had control of Dulag airfield and Tacloban airfield, and the army engineers were working on them to make them suitable for landing by American planes.

Admiral Barbey had unloaded by the end of the first day and headed back south. The second and third echelons of troops and supplies began arriving on October 22. The invasion was going very well, although it still seemed strange that the Japanese navy and Japanese air forces had not been heard from, and Leyte could not be called secure until the west side of the island was taken by Allied forces. Until then, the Japanese were free to move in troops and supplies by barge.

On October 24, General Krueger, the commander of the land forces at Leyte, set up his command post ashore and took charge of the ground forces. So the invasion of the Philippines was an established fact. It would take more than a little effort by the Japanese to dislodge the Americans now.

But the Japanese were in the process of making that enormous effort. Almost all the strength of the Japanese navy was involved, and four separate flotillas were heading for the Philippines. In fact, one of these units had already been attacked by American submarines of MacArthur's

Navy. This was Admiral Kurita's main force, and the submarines were the *Darter* and the *Dace,* operating out of Admiral Christie's command at Fremantle.

Early on the morning of October 23, the *Darter* had put four torpedoes into the Japanese cruiser *Atago,* which was Admiral Kurita's flagship. The explosions blew the ship apart, and she began to sink. Two more torpedoes, fired from the submarine's aftertubes, hit the cruiser *Takao* and blew off her rudder. Meanwhile, the submarine *Dace* had attacked the Japanese cruiser *Maya* and blown her up. So by October 24 the Japanese had already lost two major ships and seen another crippled and out of action, even before the fighting force reached the Philippines.

By this time Admiral Kinkaid was expecting a major encounter between the fleets off Leyte, and he made preparations to meet it.

On October 24 three of the carrier groups under Admiral Halsey launched search planes to look for Japanese fleet units. At eight in the morning an American carrier plane sighted the Kurita force, which was coming around Mindoro Island and heading for Tablas Strait. So Admiral Halsey ordered the carriers to launch planes and attack. But before the Americans could attack, the Japanese got in the first blow.

On the morning of October 24, planes of the Second Naval Air Fleet, conventional planes flown by conventional pilots, attacked the Americans off Leyte. In all, some three hundred Japanese planes were employed that day in a desperate effort to get at the invasion fleet. But most of them were shot down by carrier pilots, some of whom destroyed half a dozen Japanese planes. Still, one Japanese plane did get through that morning and dropped a bomb on the flight deck of the light carrier *Princeton,* which fought the damage all day long, aided by the men of other ships, but finally had to be abandoned and sunk.

The Americans got their revenge that day, however, when they' sank the battleship *Musashi,* one of the two largest in the world, and damaged the battleships *Yamato, Nagato,* and the *Haruna*. Admiral Kurita asked for air assistance from Admiral Fukudome, but he did not get it, and so he decided to turn around and move away from the San Bernardino Strait to get away from the American attack. He sailed back to the east for a few hours, but when dusk approached, he turned once more and headed into the San Bernardino Strait. The next day he planned to come around the north end of Leyte and steam down onto the invasion fleet standing off the beaches.

That evening, as the sun began to sink toward the horizon, Admiral Kurita's force was sighted by an American search plane as it headed toward the San Bernardino Strait. The admiral planned to pass through the strait at one o'clock the next morning.

Admiral Nishimura, with the Southern Force, planned to pass through Surigao Strait at four in the morning, and they expected to rendezvous a few miles north of Suluan later in the morning. Admiral Shima's smaller force was sighted at midday on October 24 near the Cagayan Islands. That morning American planes from the carriers *Enterprise* and *Franklin* sighted the Nishimura force and attacked. They bombed the battleship *Fuso* and destroyed its two float planes—the eyes of the battleship. They also wrecked the No. 1 gun turret of the destroyer *Shigure*. Other planes from the land-based air forces were sent to attack the Shima force, but as darkness closed in they could not find the Japanese ships, so the Shima force escaped air attack that day.

Admiral Kinkaid spent a busy afternoon and evening on October 24, aboard his flagship, the *Wasatch*. Word came that the airfield at Tacloban had been attacked by Japanese planes and set afire. The flames spread to a fuel dump that had just been laid down by the Americans, and that fire raged all night long.

Admiral Kinkaid was too busy to even notice. Just after noon it had become very clear that the Japanese had two groups of ships heading for Surigao Strait, hoping to move through and then to assault the Americans on the beaches. So Kinkaid ordered Admiral Oldendorf to form his ships into a disposition prepared for a night battle. There were twenty-eight Liberty ships in San Pedro Bay, as well as the cruiser *Nashville* with General MacArthur still aboard, that would be prime candidates for oblivion if the Japanese got through.

Admiral Kinkaid believed that Admiral Halsey's Third Fleet was guarding the approaches to Leyte Gulf from the north, particularly the San Bernardino Strait, so he had no worries on that score. With six battleships, four heavy cruisers, five light cruisers, and twenty-eight destroyers, Admiral Oldendorf had a strength that outweighed the Japanese by at least three to one. So as the day dwindled and darkness came, the Americans waited confidently.

17

ACTION AT SURIGAO STRAIT

After the combined attack by the American submarines *Darter* and *Dace* on Admiral Kurita's Center Striking Force on October 23, the two American submarines continued to hope for more opportunity to strike the enemy. They trailed the Japanese force all the rest of the day, surfaced at night, and planned a surface attack for October 24.

But nature took a hand. Palawan Passage, where they were operating, is only twenty-five miles at its widest point, and elsewhere it is full of shallows and rocks. Because of all the action of the past two days, both American submarines were operating on "dead reckoning," which means nothing more than a good guess at where they were. On this night they hoped to rectify this situation by getting a star fix, but when they came to the surface, the sky was covered with clouds, and they could not even get a fix on the Palawan Mountains. So they were really "flying blind" in some of the world's most dangerous and trickiest waters.

Commander D. H. McClintock, the skipper of the *Darter,* thought he knew where he was. He figured that he would pass by Bombay Shoal, a shallow that was underwater at high tide, by about seven miles. But he miscalculated, and very early on the morning of October 24 the

Darter ran hard aground right on the shoal she was trying to miss. The submarine was traveling on the surface at seventeen knots when she hit and slid up on the rocks. The noise was so tremendous that it was registered on the sound gear of the Japanese destroyers nearby, but they could not identify the source of the sound, so they did not stop to search and perhaps find the *Darter*.

Once the screeching of the steel on rock had ended, the men of the *Darter* stopped to try to figure out what had happened and what could be done. The answer was "not much," so they began burning secret documents and destroying secret military gear. Still, the captain tried to get his ship off, using all the approved tactics, of blowing ballast, rocking, and rolling. But nothing worked. They were stuck hard and fast.

The *Dace* came up and stood off the reef, trying to help. But still nothing could be done, and well before dawn both captains agreed that this was the case, so the rubber boats of the two submarines were used to bring the crew of the *Darter* onto the *Dace,* as demolition crews set charges that were supposed to blow up the *Darter*.

The charges were supposed to explode, but when dawn came and they did not, it was a matter for concern. The *Dace* tried to destroy the sister submarine with torpedoes, but all of them exploded against the reef, not on the boat. The *Dace* then tried to use her four-inch gun to destroy the boat, but by this time it was light and a Japanese plane came along and forced the submarine to dive. As they went down, up came a Japanese destroyer, and so the attempt to wreck the *Darter* had to be abandoned. The Japanese did, indeed, find the boat and go aboard her, but it did them very little good. There was no way she could be gotten off the reef without a major salvage attempt, which no one was in a position to begin just then.

The *Dace* turned homeward toward western Australia, radioing Admiral Christie. The submarine force of MacArthur's Navy had done its part in the invasion of the Philippines.

On the afternoon of October 24 Admiral Oldendorf was preparing for the battle that he expected during the night-time. Hours earlier he had been given various reports on the coming of the Japanese ships, although the reports were a bit disjointed and it was hard to figure out how many ships, and in what order they might come. He did know that a strong force was expected to appear soon. He was not sure of the enemy's disposition, but he knew that there were no aircraft carriers, and thus no special problems. This would be a night surface engagement, reminiscent of the Battle of Savo Island, but this time the Americans were making sure that there would be no such disaster as Savo, in which the United States and Australia had lost four cruisers while the Japanese got off scot-free.

Surigao Strait separates Leyte Island from Dinagat Island, with Hibuson Island in the middle and Panaon Island down about nine miles off Leyte's southern tip at Amagusan Point. The battleships were up to the northeast, off Leyte's Hingatungan Point. The cruisers were below them, moving more into the strait, and the destroyers were on the flanks to protect the big ships, and to be able to rush at the enemy for torpedo attacks as he came through the strait. The Japanese were not going to have much maneuvering room, since the strait is only twelve miles wide off Dinagat.

As Admiral Oldendorf prepared for battle, he had one worrisome problem: a shortage of armor-piercing ammunition. So quickly had the war changed that the battleships were carrying ammunition designed for shore bombardment (at Yap Island) rather than for a naval surface engagement. The battleships had enough armor-piercing ammunition aboard to shoot only five salvos at the enemy. Thereafter they would have to fire high-explosive ammunition, which would do nothing to penetrate the thick steel plates of Japanese battleships and cruisers.

As if that were not enough to worry about, Admiral Oldendorf discovered that his destroyers had only about 20 percent of the ammunition they should carry, partly because in the last few hours some of the skippers had been gun-happy and had been firing at just about anything, whether it moved or not. Nor were there any spare torpedoes for the destroyers.

But there were compensatory factors. The entrance to the strait lent itself to the use of motor torpedo boats, and Admiral Oldendorf had plenty of these, stretching through the strait and down to Camiguin Island in the Mindanao Sea: forty-eight PT boats, the mosquitoes of the fleet, which carried on their plywood hulls a deadly sting— torpedoes powerful enough to sink a warship—and whose crews were eager for accomplishment.

The PT boats had been coming in from the New Guinea area, and by the afternoon of October 24 they were ready for action. Admiral Kinkaid had already ordered them to prepare to patrol Surigao Strait just as thoroughly as possible, and the PT boat skippers knew that they were heading out to hunt big game this night. Heading south with their engines wide open, they made so much racket that sailors on the ships of the fleet got the idea that something must really be up. They had been assigned patrol sectors, ranging down the strait, and they were ready for action, thirteen sections of PT boats.

Admiral Oldendorf called a meeting of his lieutenants as dusk neared. The PT boats, he said, would be the key to the initial action. They would report on the coming of the Japanese toward the strait, and if possible they would attack the enemy and perhaps diminish his strength by damaging or sinking a ship or two.

Then, as the enemy neared the strait, the destroyers on the right flank would sally forth to make torpedo attacks, and when they had done so, the destroyers on the left flank would do the same. Twenty-eight destroyers ought to be able to create quite a lot of trouble for the Japanese force. And meanwhile, of course, as the enemy's capital ships came within range, the cruisers and battleships would be firing their guns. The fourteen- and sixteen-inch guns of the battleships, the eight-inch guns of the cruisers, and the four- and five-inch guns of the destroyers would all come into play.

The weakness of the Japanese plan to force through Surigao Strait was the split of the attack force into two separate units, neither of them strong enough to run the American gauntlet.

The first force, hours ahead of the second, was that of Admiral Nishimura. He was traveling in the battleship *Yamashiro* and had with him the damaged battleship *Fuso,* the heavy cruiser *Mogami,* and four destroyers. He was supposed to hit the strait, force through, and reach the sea off Tacloban, the center of the American invasion, at dawn on October 25. At this same time Admiral Kurita's force, led by the enormous battleship *Yamato,* was to arrive from the north, having passed through the San Bernardino Strait and sailed south along the coast of Samar and into Leyte Gulf by early morning.

Admiral Nishimura was coming along strong, bent on his mission. He did not know what he would face at Surigao Strait; perhaps he thought that he would face nothing at all. But on the evening of October 24, about an hour after Admiral Oldendorf's battle conference broke up, Admiral Nishimura had some disquieting news. He learned by message that Admiral Kurita's bigger force coming down from the north had been attacked so heavily by submarines and by American aircraft in the past few hours that it had been delayed and would not reach Tacloban—could not reach Tacloban—at the appointed hour. Nevertheless, Admiral Toyoda ordered all other units to forge ahead as planned, made no concessions because of the change in conditions, but persisted in following the plan of the Sho Operation, and Admiral Nishimura kept on coming toward Surigao Strait, still not knowing what he would find there.

"All forces will dash to the attack," said Admiral Toyoda in that nighttime message to Admiral Nishimura and the others of the Sho Operation. And so Nishimura put aside any question that might be in his mind and did what he was ordered to do. He was happy enough, in a way, because he wanted to fight a night battle. As Savo Island had proved early in the war, under certain conditions the Japanese night-fighting ability was far superior to the American. But they did not reckon with a good radar operation, which now was certainly established within the American fleet. The battle conditions of October 1944 were vastly different from those of August 1942.

An hour after Admiral Nishimura had received Admiral Youda's message to continue the attack as scheduled, he sent a message back to Tokyo, announcing that he was nearing the strait and expected to penetrate and reach a point near Dulag at four o'clock the next morning. Then, two hours later, Admiral Nishimura had a message from Admiral Kurita, changing his timetable: Kurita said that he would now reach Suluan Island at six o'clock in the morning and then go into Leyte Gulf. But that meant that he would not get into the gulf until about 11 A.M., and that was a long seven hours after Nishimura's anticipated time of arrival near Dulag.

So Nishimura kept going, but cautiously. He sent the cruiser *Mogami* and three destroyers out in front of the battleships, to see what could be seen up ahead.

Shortly before eleven o'clock that night *PT-131* was working off the island of Bohol, the next big island to the southeast of Leyte, and representing the far end of the Surigao Strait area, when she picked up radar blips representing some large ships. The leader of the section, Ensign Peter Gadd, led all three of his boats out to attack. They sped out at more than twenty-three knots, and fifteen minutes after the first report they caught sight of the two Japanese battleships a couple of miles away. Almost immediately the Japanese lookouts of the destroyer *Shigure* spotted the PT boats.

The Japanese were expert at dealing with attacks of this sort; in the battles for the Solomons they had shown that. The battleships turned toward the offending little boats, and the destroyer turned on its searchlights and soon found the three-boat flotilla. The *Shigure* began firing its guns, and *PT-131* was soon straddled. The boats sped away, making smoke to confuse the destroyer gunners. The two other boats sped off at different angles, to help with the deception. They turned and zigged and zagged, trying to keep out of range of the guns, trying also to get ready to launch a torpedo attack. But *PT-152* was caught by a Japanese shell, which blew up her 37-mm gun, and put four men of the fifteen-man crew out of action. *PT-130* was luckier. She was hit by a Japanese shell that passed right through the plywood hull without exploding, although it did knock out the radio equipment, which meant that the boat could not radio the message that the Japanese were coming. But the boat hurried along, to find the next section of PT boats up the channel, and then another boat radioed the message to Admiral Kinkaid's forces that the Japanese were on their way through Surigao Strait.

Thus just after midnight, early on October 25, Admiral Oldendorf knew, and was making ready for the fight.

The advance Japanese ships—the three destroyers and the cruiser *Mogami*—were ahead and were not seen by the PT boats as they moved along. But when the *Mogami* came by the sector assigned to the third section of PT boats, the battle cruiser was again sighted, and two of the boats fired torpedoes and then ran for cover, because a PT boat to a cruiser is like a matchstick to a timber. The three PT boats of this section ran fast, making smoke and pursued by shells from the Japanese destroyers, which came very close but did not hit any of the boats.

So Admiral Nishimura had run through almost a quarter of the PT-boat gauntlet without any damage yet. And that is how it went as the Japanese moved toward the strait: As a boat attacked, the Japanese lighted it up with searchlights, which disturbed the aim of the torpedo men, and the torpedoes all missed. The searchlights played on the boats, the Japanese destroyers fired on them, and the boats ran zigzag and making smoke to get away, and then they reported the progress of the Japanese flotilla as it moved inexorably toward the strait.

An hour after Admiral Oldendorf had settled down to wait for the enemy, Admiral Nishimura told Tokyo that he was planning to pass Panaon Island at 1:30 A.M. and then move into Leyte Gulf. He did not expect a lot of trouble. He seemed to have decided that the PT boats represented the American defenses and he had run through them without trouble. And so the cruiser *Mogami* was called and a rendezvous was made south of Limasawa Island, with two destroyers out in front, and the battleships and cruisers interspersed with the remaining destroyer behind the van.

But the Japanese had not completly run the PT-boat gauntlet, yet. Section No. 6 was patrolling off Panaon Island when the Japanese came. It was the same story: The PT boats rushed in, fired inaccurately, missed with all torpedoes, and then took a beating from the Japanese guns. On this occasion *PT-493* was hit, and so was *PT-490,* so badly that two men were killed, five were wounded, and she had to be beached. *PT-493* sank, so Admiral Nishimura was quite right when he told Admiral Toyoda that he was proceeding toward Leyte Gulf, destroying PT boats as he went.

On they went; three more PT boats came out and fired six torpedoes. All missed. The Japanese illuminated them; the PT boats ran, and successfully. No one was hurt. And it was the same all the rest of the way on the road to the strait. About thirty PT boats attacked the Japanese, but none of them scored any hits on the Nishimura force. Did anyone expect them to do so? The function of the PT boat was not to attack battleships or even destroyers, but to patrol for small craft. The PT boats had proved effective in controlling Japanese barge traffic in the Solomons and New Guinea, and they had not hesitated to take on destroyers in battle, although the results were usually dismal. This night they had performed well enough for MacArthur's Navy;

they kept Admiral Oldendorf informed all the way of the progress of the Japanese flotilla toward the strait.

And then Admiral Nishimura got a surprise. He ran into the American destroyers.

Seven of the most modern American destroyers, formed into Destroyer Squadron Fifty-four, were patrolling along the right side of the American warship disposition, waiting for the Japanese that night. They had the first report from Admiral Oldendorf about the coming of the Japanese, just after midnight, and they waited. Then, a few minutes after that first report, they learned that there was another force coming along behind Admiral Nishimura. This was Admiral Shima's unit—the heavy cruisers *Nachi* and *Ashigara,* the light cruiser *Abukuma,* and seven destroyers.

So the battle lines consisted of two Japanese battleships, three heavy cruisers, a light cruiser, and eleven destroyers heading into an American force more than three times as strong, and a force that had the extra advantage of knowing who the enemy was, where he was, and when he would arrive, while Admirals Nishimura and Shima had no idea of what they would face at Surigao Strait. The planes of Admiral Halsey's Third Fleet, in sweeping the southern Philippines clear of Japanese aircraft, had deprived the Imperial Navy of its scouting forces and its air intelligence, and in their relative weakness the Japanese were moving into almost certain disaster.

On they came in the early hours of October 25, riding a glassy sea, under a moonless sky, with visibility limited to about two miles. Just after 1 A.M. the word came to the Americans from a PT boat: The Japanese were off Panaon Island, which meant about thirty miles away from the American battle line.

Captain J. G. Coward of Destroyer Squadron Fifty-four prepared his seven ships for an attack. Two would continue on patrol, lest some enemy ship slip through the net. Five would attack with torpedoes, rushing down on the enemy before he was in range of gunfire and firing torpedoes at high speed, then turning and retiring before the big guns of the Japanese battleships could search out the destroyers.

By 2:30 that morning the Japanese were just over eighteen miles away. Admiral Nishimura had switched to battle formation, with four destroyers out in front of the two battleships and the heavy cruiser *Mogami*. The destroyers headed down on the enemy at thirty knots, and closing fast. The destroyers *Melvin, McGowan,* and *Remey* attacked first, launching twenty-seven torpedoes in short order at 3 A.M., then turned and ran away toward Surigao Strait at thirty-five knots. All around them shells began to fall, and searchlights from the Japanese battleships probed the darkness for them, but the American destroyers did not suffer even a single near miss.

And eight minutes after the firing had begun, the results showed. The battleship *Fuso* was hit by one torpedo, and immediately her speed fell. And a minute later, the American destroyers *McDermut* and *Monnsen* made their attack from the other side. The Japanese took evasive action, and that put their column right into the path of the torpedoes. In quick order the Japanese destroyers *Yamagumo, Michishio,* and *Asagumo* were hit, and so was the battleship *Yamashiro.* The *Yamagumo* blew up and sank—obviously the torpedo had set off the ship's magazine. The *Michishio* came to a dead stop and began to sink, her insides blown out. The bow of the *Asagumo* was blown off, but she was able to slow, turn around, and begin heading back for safer waters.

So five American destroyers, rushing in to conduct an attack, had scored brilliantly in the best tradition of the destroyer class; they had fired forty-seven torpedoes and hit five ships, sinking three of them. Already, although MacArthur's Navy had not yet fired its big guns, Admiral Nishimura's force was decimated, and while he put the best face he could on the event in his final message to Tokyo, he now faced total disaster.

The attack by Destroyer Squadron Fifty-four was followed ten minutes later by another destroyer attack, this by

Squadron Twenty-four. Making smoke to confuse the enemy's searchlights and gunners, six destroyers, five of them American and one Australian, headed toward the enemy. They came in just as the Japanese destroyer *Yamagumo* exploded and lit up the scene like day for their attack. This attack was not so successful. Many torpedoes missed, but one struck the battleship *Yamashiro* and slowed her down. The destroyers were now within range of their five-inch guns, and they began firing as the destroyers launched torpedoes. One or more torpedoes hit the Japanese destroyer *Michishio,* and she blew up and sank.

The Japanese ships now opened fire, and so did the American battle line behind the attacking destroyers, which turned and ran back to get out of range of their own big ships' guns. Several of these destroyers were nearly hit by Japanese gunfire.

And then just after 3:30 that morning, Admiral Oldendorf sent in his third destroyer squadron, Squadron Fifty-six, to attack the Japanese ships with torpedoes. This time nine American destroyers attacked. But by now the element of surprise was gone, and the destroyers were under heavy fire from the Japanese guns. All the torpedoes of the first three destroyers missed their targets, and they retired at high speed. The second section's torpedoes also missed, and those ships raced away.

The other three destroyers were the *Leary,* the *Newcomb,* and the *Albert W. Grant.* Two of the *Newcomb's* torpedoes found the battleship *Yamashiro,* but the Japanese gunners also ranged on the *Albert W. Grant,* and, ironically, so did the American gunners. She took eleven "friendly" shells and seven from the Japanese, and went dead in the water. (She was, however, saved. The *Newcomb* came alongside and hauled the stricken ship away to safety, and she was repaired in time for the Okinawa invasion.)

Shortly before four o'clock on the morning of October 25, the Japanese ships were in range of the Allied battleships and cruisers, and the next stage of the battle began. They did not have many targets: The Nishimura force was reduced to one battleship, one heavy cruiser, and one destroyer.

The range was about fourteen miles when the American battleships opened fire. They had the enormous advantage of being stationed across the Surigao Strait, while the enemy was coming up the strait toward them. In naval talk the result was that the Americans were able to "cap the T"—an advantage sought by sailors since before the days of Lord Nelson. All the American heavy ships were able to fire on the enemy simultaneously. And they did, particularly the battleships, five of which had been sunk at Pearl Harbor and then were raised to fight again. Today was their revenge, and they took it. Soon the *Yamashiro* was a mass of flame and exploding debris: The battleships fired nearly 280 rounds of sixteen-inch ammunition, and the cruisers fired their six- and eight-inch guns furiously (the *Columbia* alone fired 1,150 rounds).

By 4 A.M. the Nishimura force was no more. The *Yamashiro* turned around and headed back whence she had come, but ten minutes later she capsized and sank, and Admiral Nishimura went to his death. The heavy cruiser *Mogami* also turned and headed back away from the strait, trailing smoke and fire. A shell from one of the cruisers hit her bridge, killing the commanding officer and all the other officers on the bridge, and other shells slowed her down.

So the destroyer *Shigure* and the *Mogami* limped away from the scene of the carnage, passing the burning stern section of the *Fuso*, which had broken in two, as they ran.

One part of the Sho attack had been launched and had failed miserably, with only one American destroyer hit, and those hits scored mostly by its own friends in error.

Still, the battle of Surigao Strait was not yet ended. Admiral Shima's force still had to be dealt with that morning. Along they came, the cruisers *Nachi* and *Ashigara,* each capable of making thirty-six knots, and the light cruiser *Abukuma*, and that handful of destroyers. The Shima force was about an hour and a half behind the Nishimura force as it came up. They ran the gamut of the torpedo boats, but it was not much of a gamut by this time, until *PT-137* put a torpedo into the *Abukuma* by mistake (he was shooting at a destroyer at the time). Admiral Shima moved up, passed the two halves of the battered *Fuso* wreckage, and at about 4:30 A.M. decided to turn around and await developments for a while. Admiral Shima so told Tokyo and the other forces of the Sho Operation, and then he headed back down the course he had come. On the way back the *Nachi* collided with the burning *Mogami*, which then followed the Shima force in its retreat. So the Battle of Surigao Strait ended. Two battleships had been sunk, two destroyers had been sunk, and every ship of Nishimura's unit was at least damaged, the *Mogami* quite seriously, and the *Asagumo* almost as seriously.

It was a fine victory for the American "battle line" and the last surface engagement of its kind in the history of modern warfare. The next step in the battle for Leyte would be coming soon, and it would bring surprises of a different kind.

18

ONE DOWN, TWO TO GO

J ust before dawn Admiral Oldendorf learned that the battle of Surigao Strait was over, and the Japanese remnants (half a dozen) had turned around and were heading back for the Dutch East Indies bases. He sent the American destroyers to chase the enemy to try to sink the ships.

As it became light the destroyermen saw Japanese survivors in the water along their way, and when the U.S.S. *Claxton* reported that she was coming up on a group of more than a hundred survivors, she was ordered to pick up some of them, for intelligence, not humanitarian, reasons. The Japanese expected nothing and wanted nothing. In fact an officer swimming in the water ordered the men to stay clear of the boat lowered by the *Claxton,* and the boat crew had difficulty in getting any survivors at all. Finally the crew picked up three men—that was all—of 150 that the crew counted in the water. Later the ship sighted another three men in the water and tried to pick them up. One came aboard the boat without trouble, one swam away, and one had to be roped and tied and brought aboard. The tradition of never surrendering was as strong as it had ever been.

The American cruisers also set out in pursuit of the Japanese that morning, and the cruisers *Louisville, Denver,* and *Portland* found the burning cruiser *Mogami.* They fired a few shells and hit her, but they also reported that she was burning furiously, so Admiral Oldendorf ordered them to disengage and prepare for other action: He had learned that Admiral Kurita's force was coming down from the north. The *Mogami* was then trailed by a PT boat, which fired two torpedoes at the Japanese ship, but missed with both of them, and then retreated.

As the Japanese remnants under Admiral Shima headed south and west, the American PT boats became more active in the growing light. Several PT boats began to rush out to harry the retreating Japanese. *PT-194* came close enough to exchange gunfire with the cruiser *Nachi,* and the PT boat was hit by a shell, which wounded three men. *PT-190* found a column of six ships, two of the destroyers came around and opened fire on the boat, and the PT skipper wisely retired in a hurry. The Japanese then moved down toward the Mindanao shore to avoid the PT boats to the north.

Just before 7 A.M. the crew of *PT-137* sighted the burning *Mogami,* moving south at twelve knots accompanied by a destroyer. All these sighting reports prompted Admiral Oldendorf to order Rear Admiral Robert Hayler to search for stragglers and sink them, and Admiral Hayler went south with the cruisers *Denver* and *Columbia* and three destroyers. They found the Japanese destroyer *Asagumo,* which was steaming southwest painfully, its bow shot away. The men of the *Asagumo* fought valiantly, but one damaged destroyer could hardly withstand the shelling by two cruisers and three destroyers, and so she went down, the Japanese still firing their guns as the ship sank.

With no other ships in sight, the American light cruiser squadron turned around and went back to join Admiral Oldendorf's battle disposition at the mouth of Surigao Strait.

The pursuit of the fleeing Japanese ships of the Southern Force was then carried out by the planes of Admiral Sprague's escort carrier force. That morning the search planes found the Shima force and the *Mogami*, which had joined Shima, in the Mindanao Sea and began to attack with bombs and torpedoes. They hit the *Mogami* repeatedly, and her engines stopped. The destroyer *Akebono* came alongside and took off the crew, and then sank the crippled cruiser with a single torpedo.

The light cruiser *Abukuma* had been torpedoed by an American PT boat on the run toward Surigao Strait. She escaped temporarily by putting in at Dapitan, a harbor on Mindanao. For the rest of that day nobody paid much attention to that little port. Too many other things were happening up north and to the east.

For during the night of October 24, when Admiral Kinkaid was preparing MacArthur's Navy for battle with the Japanese in Surigao Strait, Admiral Halsey was remaining true to his promise that if ever he had a chance to go after the main elements (and that meant carriers and battleships) of the Japanese fleet, he would do so. Admiral Nimitz had concurred in that decision, and the provision had been written into Admiral Halsey's orders. Before the Leyte operation began, Halsey knew that he was first to hit Okinawa, Formosa, and Leyte early in October, then to support the landings on Leyte by wiping out Japanese air power in the Visaya archipelago of the Philippines, and then to give "strategic support" to the Leyte landings by destroying enemy naval and air forces in the Philippines. But if at any time the main elements of the Japanese fleet showed themselves, then Halsey's mission was to destroy that fleet.

On the afternoon of October 24 Admiral Halsey had a very good picture of the total disposition of the Japanese fleet according to the Sho plan. He knew that the Southern Force was coming into the Surigao Strait sector, and he knew that Admiral Oldendorf was there to receive them.

He knew that Admiral Kurita's force had been steaming toward the San Bernardino Strait but had turned around, and he knew that the battleship *Musashi* had been sunk and several ships damaged. But Halsey's air intelligence officers gave him one serious misconception. So many American carriers were involved in the air strikes against the Kurita force and so many enthusiastic pilots were attacking the Japanese ships that they came back with damage reports far in excess of the truth. The problem was that many of these pilots were attacking the same ships, but the combat reports gave the impression that these were different ships. Therefore Admiral Halsey had the impression that the Kurita force was very badly damaged and incapable of further trouble, which was anything but the truth.

Then, that afternoon, Halsey learned of the presence of the Ozawa force of carriers and other warships off Luzon Island. When he had the reports of the carriers in the Ozawa force, Halsey began to think again of the alternatives. It was time to go out to destroy the Japanese fleet, he decided.

And so, as the Southern Force steamed toward its disaster at Surigao Strait, Admiral Halsey was assembling his fleet units off Luzon, gathering them for a run that would put them within striking distance of the Japanese carrier force in the morning. There was a moment's thought about what should be done with the fast battleship force of the Third Fleet, but Halsey decided to take it with him to the north, in case a surface action should prove possible, instead of leaving the battleships to guard against a possible incursion by the Japanese surface forces by way of the San Bernardino Strait. And Halsey did not tell Admiral Kinkaid what he was doing.

In terms of authority, there was no reason why Admiral Halsey should have informed Admiral Kinkaid of his move. Halsey was under the command of Admiral Nimitz, and Kinkaid was under the command of General MacArthur.

But had Halsey indicated that he was moving his whole fleet away from the San Bernardino Strait, Admiral Kinkaid might have taken different action. As it was, Kinkaid did nothing in particular in his confidence that all the avenues of entrance to Leyte Gulf were protected.

And so, just after midnight on October 25, when the Kurita force came out through the San Bernardino Strait and turned down the coast of Samar Island, heading for Leyte Gulf, there was nobody there to stop it.

Admiral Kurita moved his ships into four columns and came steaming down at twenty knots. On the east, or outside, was the destroyer screen, led by the light cruiser *Noshiro*. Next to the destroyers were the heavy cruisers *Kumano, Suzuya, Chikuma,* and *Tone*. Next to them were the heavy cruisers *Haguro* and *Chokai*, and next to them was another line of destroyers, led by the light cruiser *Yahagi*. Then, behind the *Haguro* and *Chokai* was the superbattleship *Yamato,* with her 18-inch guns, and the battleship *Nagato,* with 16-inch guns. Behind the *Kumano* cruiser column were the older battleships *Kongo* and *Haruna*. It was a formidable force, and one that would have caused Admiral Oldendorf concern if he had been asked to oppose it with his old battleships and cruisers and destroyers of MacArthur's Navy. But of course, since Admiral Kinkaid did not know of Admiral Halsey's departure with the the Third Fleet, no such instructions were given to Admiral Oldendorf.

At Clark Field, at Mabalacat, and at airfields on Cebu and Negros, Japanese army and navy planes prepared for the next day's action. So far Admiral Ohnishi's Kamikaze units had not enjoyed any successes; the plane that struck the *Australia* that day was an army plane. All the Kamikaze units had encountered bad weather, and none had found the enemy ships. Admiral Fukudome's Second Air Fleet had made its supreme effort against Halsey's carriers, and for the loss of some three hundred planes had only the fluke sinking of the carrier *Princeton* by a single 500-

pound bomb to show. That night, Admiral Fukudome had very little left with which to operate, and he came around to Admiral Ohnishi's views about the need to employ suicide tactics. So that night the naval air force fliers were preparing to dash forth the next day to make the supreme sacrifice for Emperor and country.

19

THE BATTLE OFF SAMAR

As Admiral Kurita's 12 battleships and cruisers and their accompanying destroyers steamed south to attack the American forces at Leyte Gulf, the only major ships standing between them and the beaches of Leyte and the transports off the shore were the escort carriers of Admiral Thomas Sprague.

"Only" is not a very good word to describe the escort carrier force, for it consisted of 16 carriers, 21 destroyers, and 444 fighting aircraft, about twice as many as the Japanese had in the Philippines at the moment. But "only" indicates the attitude that existed then and still persists about the value of the escort carrier force during World War II. A plane from an escort carrier could carry just as powerful bombs and torpedoes as planes from fleet carriers and could deliver them in the same way. The real difference, aside from the number of planes carried by each small carrier, was the vulnerability of the ship. The men who sailed the escort carriers called them "coffins," because in their construction some safety precautions had been sacrificed to convenience and speed of building. And, of course, at eighteen knots they were not nearly so fast as the fleet carriers, which could make more than thirty knots. But the escort carrier force was a formidable

weapon, and on this day above all others, that truth would
be shown to the world.

On the morning of October 25 Admiral Thomas
Sprague's force was divided into three groups, called "taffies." Two of the carriers had left the day before for refuel-
ing and rearmament. Taffy One was operating in the south,
off Mindanao, and that morning its search planes were out
tracking the defeated Southern Force that had been battered at Surigao Strait. About fifty miles to the northeast,
off the entrance to Leyte Gulf, was Taffy Two, and fifty
miles north of that group, off the southern coast of Samar
Island, was Taffy Three.

The Japanese saw the Americans first. At 6:44 that
morning, a masthead lookout aboard the battleship *Yamato*
reported several American carriers to the southeast of the
speeding Japanese ships. A single torpedo bomber bearing
American markings headed toward the ships, and the
Japanese antiaircraft gunner opened fire. Meanwhile the
gunnery officers prepared to start firing on the American
ships to the south of them.

That morning, Admiral Kinkaid had ordered a routine air
search to the north of Leyte, but it was late in getting off,
and so Admiral Kurita had kept steaming south, un-
detected.

Taffy One was bent on chasing the ships of Admiral
Shima, and its planes were moving off the decks of those
carriers. At 5:30 that morning Taffy Three, off Samar,
launched a combat air patrol of twelve fighter planes to
watch over the ships in and around Leyte Gulf. Half an
hour later four torpedo bombers and two more fighters
went off on antisubmarine patrol. And then the crews of
the ships settled down to breakfast and relaxation, as usual,
after launching planes on a routine day.

And then, just after quarter to seven that morning,
everything seemed to happen at once.

The pilot of one of the antisubmarine patrol bombers
reported that he was attacking a Japanese warship, and

that there were four battleships, eight cruisers, and many destroyers just where he was at the moment. The report got to Admiral Sprague, who thought the pilot was attacking an American ship of Admiral Halsey's fleet and so warned.

But aboard the carrier *Fanshaw Bay* the radarmen reported a ship contact where there should be no ship. The radiomen thought that they heard somebody talking in Japanese on the fighter plane radio circuit. And someone saw antiaircraft fire up north and wondered who was shooting at what.

A pilot aboard the *Gambier Bay*, the carrier farthest north in Taffy Three got up from breakfast in the wardroom and stepped out on the flight deck for a bit of air. He looked up to the north.

"Keerist," he said, "look at those pagodas. . . ."

He was referring to the odd pagoda-shaped masts of several ships up north, shapes that every pilot knew were peculiar to Japanese battleships and cruisers.

And just at that moment, varicolored splashes began to appear in the water around the carrier *Gambier Bay*, each color the mark of one of the Japanese ships, which were attacking, firing salvos, and seeking the range.

It was 6:58 in the morning. Three minutes later, Admiral Clifton A. F. Sprague, the commander of Taffy Three, ordered a call for help made in the clear to all American vessels. If any of Admiral Halsey's task groups were about, he wanted their immediate assistance. But the fact was that Halsey's ships were far to the northeast, preparing to engage the carriers and other ships of Admiral Ozawa's "bait" force. In this aspect, the Sho Operation was a complete success; Ozawa had been sent out to lure Admiral Halsey away from the Philippines while Admirals Kurita, Nishimura, and Shima wiped out the Leyte invasion forces. And there Ozawa was, with Halsey hot on his tail.

Admiral Clifton Sprague could not depend on anyone but himself and his fellow escort carrier admirals and the destroyers and escorts of the screen that morning. Halsey was gone, Oldendorf was too far away. There was nobody around to help him.

He ordered full speed, which was almost eighteen knots, and he ordered that every plane possible be launched to fight the enemy, and he ordered his ships to make smoke to conceal the little carriers from the Japanese.

The Japanese just then were about seventeen miles north of the American carrier group.

Admiral Clifton Sprague had a real problem. The Japanese battleships were much faster than his escort carriers, and to run was simply to prolong the inevitable. He changed the course of Taffy Three so that the ships were heading due east. This put them almost into the wind, at least close enough to launch planes from the decks of the carriers without changing course. This was just about the only good luck he had.

No, there was one other bit: The weather that morning was calm, with a light breeze and a high humidity that let the smoke that the ships made as they ran hover close above the water and conceal their movements from the enemy.

The message in the clear that Admiral Clifton Sprague had sent was partly aimed at any fleet carriers about, but also at Admiral Oldendorf's battleships and cruisers. They were at the mouth of Leyte Gulf, a long way away, but Sprague could hope.

The message also alerted all the other escort carriers, even those of Admiral Thomas Sprague, down off Mindanao, and within minutes every carrier was launching planes that would head for the battle area to try to rout the Japanese.

Even as Admiral Kurita's ships began firing on the American northern escort carrier group, Admiral Kurita was worried. His lookouts had reported American carriers, and the admiral did not really differentiate between carriers as much as the Americans did. To him a carrier was a carrier and deadly because of the sting of its planes. He had already lost the *Musashi,* that superbattleship that was supposed to be unsinkable, to carrier planes on the day before. Admiral Kurita ordered the ships to attack as they wished, instead of keeping them in a battle formation. Consequently the Japanese ships began to string out.

Admiral Clifton Sprague had six little carriers, the *Fanshaw Bay,* the *St. Lo,* the *White Plains,* the *Kalinin Bay,* the *Kitkun Bay,* and the *Gambier Bay,* and three destroyers and four destroyer escorts to protect them, mostly from submarine attack, it had seemed before. Now the need had changed drastically.

The six carriers formed into a circle, about a mile and a half in circumference, and the destroyers and escorts patrolled around the perimeter. The carriers worked frantically, getting their first line of defense off the decks, the fighter planes and torpedo planes and bombers that could threaten the Japanese ships.

Just after seven o'clock the battle was becoming truly furious. Admiral Clifton Sprague saw splashes around his whole formation. The Japanese were not hitting yet, but they were moving in, salvo after salvo, with alarming precision. The admiral ordered his destroyers and escorts to begin launching torpedo attacks on the enemy.

Rear Admiral Ralph Ofstie was in command of two of the carriers, the *Kitkun Bay* and the *Gambier Bay.* The *Kitkun Bay* immediately put up eleven fighters and six torpedo bombers. Commander R. L. Fowler, the leader of the ship's air group, also flew off and moved up to the Japanese fleet, where he began circling and directing air attacks on the Japanese ships. This was a most difficult job, because the planes from various small carriers were coming in from all sides, in twos and threes, and to make them get together to coordinate their attacks was very hard. At first, the planes simply arrived and began shooting, one by one.

For a while it seemed that matters were going to improve for the Americans. Admiral Clifton Sprague turned south, to move toward the mouth of Leyte Gulf and the Oldendorf protective force there. Admiral Kurita kept on his course, to maintain the weather gauge, which meant the assistance of the wind, and so he was steering east. The distance between the Japanese and the Americans began to widen, and the Japanese shooting became less accurate. The splashes around the ships got farther away. A rain squall came along to envelop the American ships, and this helped.

The destroyers around the Sprague carrier group were ordered to attack first. They were the *Hoel,* the *Heermann* and the *Johnston.* The *Johnston* went first—she was closest to the Japanese, about ten miles away. The *Johnston* ran toward the Japanese, laying a smoke screen as she went. Her five-inch guns began to fire at the cruiser *Kumano,* and they fired 200 rounds, scoring several hits. She ran in at twenty-five knots, got to a point about five miles from the *Kumano,* and fired ten torpedoes. She would have fired more, but ten was all she had aboard. She turned with an enormous spurt and began running back behind her own smoke. Inside the smoke, the men of the *Johnston* could not see what was happening up Japanese way, but they heard: At the appointed moment when the torpedoes were supposed to begin hitting, they heard at least two, and maybe three, underwater explosions. And then when they came out of the smoke, looking back, they could see the cruiser *Kumano* burning and slowing down.

Meanwhile, the planes of the escort carrier force had arrived over the Japanese fleet and were buzzing around like angry bees defending their hives. Some of the bombers were loaded with torpedoes, the result of the foresight of Captain R. F. Whitehead, Admiral Kinkaid's air officer, who had ordered torpedoes for the morning flights in the chance that they would be used against the Japanese ships retreating out of Surigao Strait. But many of the planes that arrived over the Kurita fleet were armed with bombs, because it was much simpler and quicker to load bombs than torpedoes, which took a lot of adjusting and checking. And some of the bombers were not armed with anything but their machine guns, because they had gotten off the decks in a hurry to make way for other planes.

But no matter what the American pilots had aboard, they used it that morning. The "bees" buzzed over the Japanese fleet, their very lack of coordination adding to the general effect and confusing the Japanese gunners and the steering. They began scoring hits. As the destroyer *Johnston* retired, her captain, Commander Ernest E. Evans, seemed to have scored first against the enemy, but in fact he had not. Already the cruiser *Suzuya* had been bombed by some of those "bees," and the damage was severe enough to reduce her speed to twenty knots.

But the effect of the *Johnston*'s brave attack was immediate and visible. The *Kumano* slowed to a stop, burning furiously. The admiral of the cruiser division, Vice-Admiral K. Shiraishi, shifted his command to the *Suzuya*, and then he discovered the damage to that ship, too, and the two cruisers turned around and moved away from the battle, out of the fight. Indeed, the Americans had scored first blood.

It was too much to expect that a destroyer could run up to within five miles of an entire Japanese fleet and escape unscathed. A few minutes after the *Johnston* came out of the smoke, she was hit by three fourteen-inch shells from one of the old Japanese battleships, and the damage crews had not even gotten into action before she was hit again by three six-inch shells from a Japanese light cruiser. The effect was disastrous. The aft fire-room and engine room were instantaneously destroyed. The steering lost all power. The electrical connections to the aft five-inch guns were knocked out and so they could not fire, and the compass was destroyed. Three officers were killed on the bridge. All of Commander Evans's clothes above the waist were blown off, and he lost two fingers on one hand. From the bridge he could see enormous holes in his decks below, and he could only estimate how many men had been killed by those six shells, which had arrived within thirty seconds. The ship slowed to seventeen knots, but the *Johnston* was not out of the battle.

The steering was changed to manual. The gun stations went on manual operation, too. She plunged into the rain squall and for the next ten minutes was safe, out of sight, while Commander Evans tried to restore the ship's fighting ability. She emerged from the mist, her guns firing, and was back in the battle.

The second American destroyer to attack Kurita's ships was the U.S.S. *Hoel*. Her captain was Commander L. S. Kintberger. Her target was the Japanese battleship *Kongo*.

The *Hoel* headed toward the battleship, and both ships opened fire. Just before 7:30 the *Hoel* was hit on the bridge, and the voice radio system was broken. The destroyer then launched four torpedoes at the *Kongo,* but they all missed. Then the *Hoel* began taking many hits from the battleship's shells, until one engine failed. She kept fighting and launched more torpedoes, this time at the cruiser *Haguro,* which was leading the Japanese cruiser column. These torpedoes may have hit home. No one could ever tell for sure, because the ships involved were all lost, and so were the records. Survivor stories were the only clues.

The *Heermann* then got into the fight. Her captain, Commander Amos T. Hathaway, ordered torpedoes fired at the cruiser *Haguro,* which missed, but so did the fifteen salvos of gunfire that the cruiser aimed at the destroyer.

The *Heermann* then changed course and headed down on four battleships. At 8 A.M. she fired three torpedoes at the battleship *Haruna,* and the men aboard the destroyer thought that they got one hit. So many torpedoes were being fired by the American destroyers that the Japanese were having trouble evading them. The *Yamato* got caught between two spreads of torpedoes, one on each side, and had to reverse course and run away from the battle for ten minutes before the torpedoes ran down.

The *Hoel,* operating on only one engine, now became the prime target for the Japanese battleships and cruisers. She kept fighting, however, firing her five-inch guns, although she was taking hits constantly. Finally it was estimated that she had been hit forty times, by shells ranging from five-inch to sixteen-inch. They passed so close to the *Yamato* that the men of the *Hoel* could see the Japanese sailors on the decks.

At 8:30 a shell from a cruiser knocked out the one remaining engine, and the *Hoel* skidded to a stop. The magazine was on fire, the engine rooms were full of water, and the ship was sinking. The crew abandoned ship, and the Japanese kept firing at her as she sank.

The *Heermann* was hit repeatedly by shells from the cruiser *Chikuma.* That cruiser turned away, but the cruiser *Tone* began firing at the *Heermann* and scoring hits. But the destroyer kept firing and also laying smoke to screen the carriers behind her.

The planes from the carriers continued buzzing around the *Tone,* and the cruiser soon retired from the battle and sailed away from the scene. Still the Japanese cruiser column was gaining on the little carriers, so the *Johnston* now came out of the smoke and engaged the leading Japanese cruisers, which were very close. The Japanese then ordered their own destroyers to make a torpedo attack, and they came on, while the cruiser *Haguro* turned away to give them room for action.

The Japanese destroyers and the cruiser all launched torpedoes, but they were too far from the aircraft carriers to hit. One torpedo was exploded by gunfire from an American torpedo bomber, and another was hit by a shell from the carrier *St. Lo* and blew up. The Japanese destroyers then concentrated their five-inch gunfire on the *Johnston,* and soon the ship was a wreck. At 9:45 she was abandoned, and half an hour later she sank.

The destroyer escort *Samuel B. Roberts* also made a torpedo attack on the Japanese. She came up to within three miles of the Japanese cruisers and launched three torpedoes. They all missed.

The escort *J. C. Butler* attacked, and so did the *Raymond*. The *Raymond* launched three torpedoes at the *Haguro,* but they all missed—largely because the Japanese captains were very good at taking evasive action. The *Dennis* launched torpdoes at the cruiser *Chokai,* and they missed.

But all this activity was giving the Japanese a hard time, and when it was combined with a constant attack of fighter and bomber planes, strafing and bombing and dropping torpedoes, it became very discouraging to the Japanese captains. The total absence of any Japanese air cover was equally discouraging.

Such a battle could not go on for long. By 10 A.M. all the escorts but one had expended all their torpedoes, and the destroyers, too, were either sunk or out of torpedoes. The escorts were also under fire. The *Dennis* was hit by several shells, and she had to retire. The *Samuel B. Roberts* was hit many many times, and she was abandoned and sank.

But all this frantic activity by the escorts had done what the destroyermen wanted: It had given the carriers more time and had served to discourage the Japanese from bearing down on them.

While the cruisers and the front line of battleships were engaging the American destroyers, the *Nagato,* the *Yamato,* and several cruisers were turning their attention to the American aircraft carriers.

The *Kalinin Bay* was hit as she was launching her fighter planes just before 8 A.M. And then she was hit again, but meanwhile the men at the single five-inch gun that the ship carried had scored a hit on the cruiser that was shooting at them. Not that it stopped the cruiser, not at all, but it gave the men of the *Kalinin Bay* a great deal of satisfaction to shoot back.

The two carriers closest to the enemy and thus most vulnerable were the *Kalinin Bay* and the *Gambier Bay.* But the *Fanshaw Bay* was hit four times, and the *White Plains* was also hit. Ultimately the *Kalinin Bay* got hit by one shell from a battleship, plus thirteen from the cruisers. But she did not go down, and she kept formation all the while.

Yes, the "jeep" carriers really performed on this twenty-fifth day of October, 1944, and showed that although they might not be constructed for optimum safety, they could get along.

The unlucky ship was the carrier *Gambier Bay*. She was closest of all to the enemy, and she took the brunt of the attack by the Japanese cruisers. The shells began searching her out just before eight that morning. She was hit first at 8:10 on the flight deck, and after that it was just one shell after another as the Japanese found and kept the range. By 8:45 she was dead in the water, with her radar out, all control gone, and the engine rooms flooded. The firing was so intense that when the order was given to abandon ship and men began to go over into the water, some of them were killed in the water by shell fragments from the Japanese cruisers. Shortly after 9 A.M. the *Gambier Bay* capsized.

But while the Japanese sank this carrier and two destroyers and one escort, they did not come away at all happily from this encounter. The really effective weapon against them and the one that defeated Admiral Kurita, was the air power generated by that force of escort carriers. Although Commander Fowler, up above, had difficulty in organizing attacks, the planes did attack, and they did cause serious damage to the Japanese fleet. The ships were hit by bombs and torpedoes, and they were repeatedly strafed. Finally, with so many carriers in sight, and so little success so far, and so many planes buzzing about and no Japanese aircraft or any hope of seeing them, Admiral Kurita decided that he would have to withdraw, and shortly after 9 A.M. Admiral Kurita ordered his captains to break off the action and head north. The escort carriers had stopped the Japanese fleet!

Admiral Kurita milled around the area for several hours, waiting. Perhaps the Ozawa force would arrive to help. Perhaps the Nishimura and Shima forces would come. He did not know what had happened to any of them, and in the complete failure of communications, he had only his hopes. But the planes kept after him, and he finally decided that there was nothing more he could do here except lose more ships. Therefore he started back toward the San Bernardino Strait. And so at noon, Admiral Kurita sent a message to Tokyo, announcing that he was abandoning the strike against Leyte. This decision was covered by another; saying that Kurita was heading north to try to find the main elements of the American fleet and defeat them decisively, but that was all window dressing. The American fleet (Halsey) was nowhere within reach, and it was lucky for Kurita that this was so. Kurita wanted to get out of there and stop the stinging of those bees, so he did. The Battle of Samar came to an end, and the American beachhead of the Leyte invasion was saved from disaster by those escort carriers, which had served so well this day.

In the controversy that developed within the navy and with historians over the rectitude of Admiral Halsey's decision to seek out the carrier elements of the Japanese fleet instead of guarding the San Bernardino Strait, the story of Admiral Clifton Sprague's escort carrier force has been submerged for years, and the escort carriers have never gotten the recognition that they deserve. The day of that sort of battle is now long gone, and such tales are relegated to the history books, but the escort carriers, designed primarily to fight submarines in the Atlantic, proved a new usefulness this day in fighting off major elements of the Japanese fleet.

20
KAMIKAZE!

The reason why Admiral Kurita did not see any Japanese planes above to protect him from the American fighters and bombers on October 25 was that there were very few Japanese planes left operational in the Philippines on that day. And what was left was now going into a new phase of air operations, the suicide attack.

Admiral Ohnishi had organized his suicide forces, and they had been waiting for weather reasonable enough to launch an attack. The lack of search planes in the Philippines meant that they had difficulty keeping track of the movements of the American carrier fleet, and the carriers were the focus of Admiral Ohnishi's plans. On this morning nine suicide planes were taking off to find the American fleet, each of them escorted by a fighter pilot in another plane, who would report on the success or failure of the suicide mission.

Several of these planes did find the American fleet, although what they found was not the Halsey fleet that they wanted, but the escort carrier fleet, strung out from Mindanao to Samar.

Admiral Thomas Sprague's Taffy One—the carriers *Sangamon, Suwannee, Santee,* and *Petrof Bay* and eight escorts—were operating off Mindanao, far out of the way of Admiral Kurita's Center Force's attack off Samar.

Early that morning the little carriers launched a scouting force of seventeen fighter planes and eleven bombers to try to find the Japanese forces that had attacked toward Surigao Strait the night before. But then, an hour after these planes were launched, Admiral Sprague had the message from Admiral Clifton Sprague up north that he was under attack by the Kurita force, and so everything was halted, and the move to help stop Kurita began.

The carrier *Santee* was recovering planes from the early morning mission just before eight o'clock that morning of October 25 when suddenly out of the cloud cover appeared six Japanese planes. One came out of a cloud, headed purposefully for the carrier, machine guns spitting, and before the antiaircraft guns could be brought to bear on it, the plane crashed into the flight deck and continued down through the hangar deck. The explosion of the bomb fitted to the fighter plane ripped a hole fifteen feet wide and a hundred and thirty feet long and killed sixteen men and injured twenty-seven.

Another plane then peeled off and came in toward the carrier *Suwannee*. The gunners of that carrier opened fire and hit the plane, which trembled and then headed for the *Sangamon*. This plane was hit again by the gunners of the *Suwannee* and shot down before it could crash into the *Sangamon*. By this time the men of the carriers knew that they faced a new weapon. These were not the actions of pilots whose planes had been damaged, or who had been so badly wounded that they knew they were going to die, anyhow. These were purposeful dives to try to crash the planes into the ships, and the Americans did not need Tokyo Rose to tell them that they were facing a new weapon in this war.

A third Kamikaze came barreling in toward the *Petrof Bay,* but it, too, was shot down by antiaircraft fire.

That day the dangers came from above and below as well. The *Santee's* crew had just put out the fires caused by the Kamikaze when the ship was hit by a torpedo fired by the Japanese submarine *I-56*. This blow caused more damage, but not enough to put the carrier out of action. She could still make sixteen knots.

The carrier *Suwannee* took a Kamikaze aboard that day, too. It was one of three Japanese Zeros that came in together. The gunners shot down two of them, but the third crashed into the flight deck, doing considerable damage, but again not enough to keep the carrier from operating.

That was the extent of the Kamikaze operations around Mindanao that day, but other Kamikazes from Luzon were coming in to attack the ships of the escort force off Samar.

The pilots of these planes had been briefed by Admiral Ohnishi, who had spent a lot of time devising a method of attack by Kamikaze pilots to be most effective. The technique consisted of flying very low on the water on the approach to the ships, so as to avoid the radar and also the eyes of spotters, and then when inside the range of the spotting radar, suddenly to climb to about five thousand feet altitude and then dive down on the ships. The technique also minimized the effectiveness of the antiaircraft guns, cutting the interval during which the planes were vulnerable.

The pilots of the five planes from Luzon had learned their lessons well, and they followed the Ohnishi technique to the letter. They got inside the screen and avoided the combat air patrol and suddenly were hurtling down on the carriers.

Admiral Ofstie's flagship, the *Kitkun Bay*, was the first one of Taffy Three to get hit. The Zero that attacked this ship aimed for the bridge but missed, passed over the island, crashed into the port catwalk, and bounced into the sea. These earliest Kamikaze planes consisted of an aircraft with a bomb lashed to the fuselage. This particular bomb shook off during the bounce from the catwalk and exploded aboard the ship, doing a lot of damage.

Two more planes headed for the *Fanshaw Bay*, but both were shot down by the expert American antiaircraft gunners. Two more dove on the *White Plains* and were taken under fire by the 40-mm antiaircraft guns. One of them was hit badly. It turned and crashed into the *St. Lo,* the next ship in formation. The plane smashed through the flight deck and burst into flames on the hangar deck. The *Santee* had just had the same experience, with the bomb narrowly missing the ship's bomb and torpedo storage compartments. The *St. Lo* was not so lucky. The Kamikaze started fires belowdecks, and these spread quickly and enveloped the torpedo storage area. They spread to the bomb area. In a few moments a whole section of flight deck came hurtling upward, and seven distinct explosions were heard, as general conflagration of the flight deck made it look as though the carrier was sinking and burning up. But the fact was that the damage control parties were very effective, and the flames that day were extinguished.

On the basis of the information that Admiral Ohnishi had from his pilots, he went to Admiral Fukudome, and they agreed that the suicide system was the only avenue left to the Japanese navy in the Philippines. Thereafter, the suicide mission became standard for navy planes. On October 27, Ohnishi moved the target area to Leyte, and thereafter the suicide planes concentrated on that area.

The Kurita force headed for home waters but was pursued, again by the planes of the escort carriers. The planes dropped bombs on the battleship *Nagato* and on the cruiser *Tone*. On October 26, the Kurita force was moving into Tablas Strait, and they battered the cruiser *Noshiro* and the cruiser *Kumano*. These two were later sunk. Land-based planes of MacArthur's air force also battered the *Nagato* and the *Kongo*. The destroyer *Hayashimo* was hit and beached. The destroyer *Shiranuhi* was hit and sunk.

Day after day, more ships from the Japanese foray into the Philippines were found and sunk. On October 27, American planes sank the destroyer *Fujinami*. Planes and destroyers attacked Japanese submarines in Leyte Gulf, and the destroyers sank the *I-45* and *I-46*.

In the last few days of October, Admiral Ohnishi's Kamikazes also scored more heavily against the American fleet. The carrier *Intrepid* was hit by a Kamikaze on October 29, and the *Franklin* was hit again, and so was the *Belleau Wood* damaged by a Kamikaze. *Belleau Wood*'s damage was more or less typical of the carriers' losses: She lost twelve planes and ninety-two crewmen in that one crash.

At the end of October, Admiral Ohnishi had great hopes for his program to stop the American advance in the Philippines, and with some reason. The Japanese had begun staging aircraft into the islands from the Japanese aircraft factories, which were still producing thousands of planes every month.

By November 1, Admiral Ohnishi was prepared to make a major effort at Leyte Gulf, and the army was conducting some ordinary air raids at the same time. On that day, the destroyer *Claxton* was severely damaged by a Kamikaze, and so was the destroyer *Ammen*. The destroyer *Killen* was bombed by a conventional bomber and damaged, and the destroyer *Bush* was attacked eight times during that morning but managed to evade all attacks. The destroyer *Abner Read* was sunk that day by a Kamikaze that crashed through its deck. The destroyer *Anderson* was bombed.

This series of attacks brought about retaliation from the Americans in the form of a series of air strikes on the airfields by the Third Fleet's planes. Admiral Kinkaid called for help, and he got it. Admiral Halsey began a whole new round of air strikes against the airfields he had hit so many times before. At that time the cruiser *Reno* was hit by a torpedo from a submarine, and she had to be taken back to the base at Ulithi for repairs.

Halsey's planes scoured the Philippine airfields and almost always found some real planes to destroy among the many dummies on the fields. But the supply did not cease. The planes were staged down daily from Kyushu Island, and although many were lost by inexperienced pilots, many also got through. So Admiral Ohnishi and his army counterparts had a constantly replenished supply of suicide planes to throw against MacArthur's Navy and the Americans ashore. The Halsey forces also got hit. The *Lexington* was struck by a Kamikaze on November 5, and lost 150 men, with 132 injured. But the American air strikes again cut down the number of planes available.

The zigzag war continued: The Japanese assembled planes and made a series of Kamikaze attacks; the Americans slashed back with raids on all the airfields, and the same pattern was repeated. The Third Fleet, cruising around the Philippines, kept waking hits on Japanese convoys and destroyers as they tried to bring reinforcements to Leyte. So the fighting continued on in November.

Admiral Halsey had planned to take the Third Fleet from the Philippines to strike Japan in November. But in the first week of that month Admiral Nimitz sent Rear Admiral Forrest P. Sherman to Tacloban, where General MacArthur and Admiral Kinkaid had established headquarters, and the general and his admiral objected very strenuously to the Halsey plans. The problem was that the Leyte airfields had to be rebuilt by the engineers before army planes could use them, and this had not been completed. And the planes of the Third Fleet, as well as those of the escort carriers, were needed to supply defense against the Kamikaze units. Reluctantly Admiral Halsey canceled his plans to head for Japanese home waters and went back to the task of trying to control Japanese air power in the Philippines.

But it was no easy task. On November 16, Admiral Ohnishi launched a new Kamikaze offensive in Leyte Gulf.

The transports *Alpine* and *James O'Hara* were hit by suicide planes within a few days. On November 27, Kamikazes went after the big carrier task force groups once again, and two hit the cruiser *St. Louis.* The battleship *Maryland* was hit by a Kamikaze, as were the destroyers *Aulick* and *Saufley,* and then the *Drayton* was hit, and the *Mugford.*

MacArthur's Navy staged a new amphibious landing at Ormoc, on the far side of Leyte. The troops were landed by Admiral Struble, under the general command of Admiral Barbey. The soldiers were men of the Seventy-seventh Division, under Major General A. D. Bruce. The landings were made successfully on December 7, 1944, but within hours Admiral Ohnishi's Kamikazes were over the beaches, spreading their particular sort of havoc. The destroyer *Mahan* was hit by three Kamikazes within about five minutes, and they sank her. Three Kamikazes attacked the destroyer *Ward,* and one hit her squarely and sank her. Three other destroyers were almost immediately attacked, but they managed to shoot down all of the suicide planes and escape unhurt. The destroyer *Liddle* was hit, and her captain, Lieutenant Commander L. C. Brogger, was killed. That day the destroyer *Lamson* was also hit by a Kamikaze that killed twenty-one men and wounded fifty.

The American navy, by this time, was very conscious of the Kamikazes, and Admiral Nimitz was concerned because his ships and those of MacArthur's Navy were taking the worst beating they had suffered since the earliest days of Guadalcanal. The successes of the Kamikazes were largely veiled from the American people, so concerned were the naval authorities. But the battle for Leyte continued and the Allies were winning it. Army air force and navy planes, and destroyers and submarines, exacted their toll of the Japanese resupply convoys that tried to bring men and food and ammunition to Leyte.

In the second week of December, MacArthur's Navy began running resupply convoys around Leyte, from the original landing area to Ormoc Bay on the other side. The

first of these on December 8, was escorted by Destroyer
Squadron Fifty-six and consisted of a dozen LSMs (landing
ship medium) and four LCIs.

The Japanese answer was still more suicide missions. On
December 10 the Kamikazes made for Surigao Strait,
where there was always Allied naval activity. A twin-
engined bomber dived into the destroyer *Hughes* and inflicted twenty-three casualties. The Liberty ship *William S.
Ladd* was also hit by a Kamikaze and later sank. An LCT
and a PT boat were also sunk this day.

The resupply of the American forces continued, and the
troops moved to wedge the Japanese into a corner of Leyte.
On December 11, another convoy from MacArthur's Navy
set out with eight LCMs and four LCIs. Six destroyers
provided the sea escort, and the convoy was covered in the
air by Marine fighters. But there were only four of these
fighters, and the convoy's commander complained that this
was not enough, given the methods of the Kamikaze pilots.

He was quite right. At five o'clock on the evening of
December 11, ten Kamikazes came in to attack. One
crashed very close to the destroyer *Reid*, shot down by
antiaircraft guns, so close that it started a fire on the ship. A
second exploded over the ship. Then, one of the escorting
pilots, whose mission was to report on the successes of the
Kamikazes, dropped a bomb, which missed, and a fourth
plane came in and crashed on the port side. The *Reid*
turned over on her beam ends and sank. The ship's maga-
zines then exploded, underwater, and the explosion killed
many crewmen who were struggling in the water. In all
only about a hundred and fifty men, or half the ship's crew,
were saved.

The action around Leyte was constant and vigorous.
That same day the destroyer *Caldwell* shot down two Kamikazes, was threatened by a third, which was shot down by
an American fighter plane, and escaped only shaken up.
The Ormoc supply mission was a success. At the same time
the Japanese were trying to do the same, and they sent two

destroyers and a barge to that area. American destroyers and PT boats and planes combined to sink the destroyers *Uzuki* and *Suzuki* that night. The American convoy started back for Leyte Gulf, but as dawn came, it was attacked by a new group of Kamikazes. Three dove on the destroyer *Caldwell*, one crashed, and seventy-three men were killed or wounded. That day the Marine Corps planes overhead shot down eleven Japanese planes, but the problem was that Admiral Ohnishi and the army authorities just kept on sending in more suicide missions, and they never seemed to cease.

Still, MacArthur's Navy was doing its job, and the invasion was succeeding, if not quite so rapidly as the general had hoped. General MacArthur had wanted to make a landing on the island of Mindoro, about two hundred and fifty miles north of Leyte Island in the first week of December, but the strength of the Kamikaze operations was so great just then that Admiral Kinkaid objected, and General Kenney, the commander of the Fifth Army Air Force, agreed. They said that the Kamikazes had to be gotten under control first. So the Mindoro operation had been postponed until December 15. By that time, although there was no cessation of the Kamikaze attacks, MacArthur's Navy had to move the troops up. Palompon on Leyte was captured, and the battle for that island was very nearly over. General MacArthur so indicated on December 16, and General Yamashita, the Japanese commander in the Philippines, concurred, on Christmas Day, when he told the troops on Leyte that they were on their own: Yamashita would concentrate his defense on Luzon Island.

21

TO LUZON

E ven as the fighting continued on Leyte and the
men of the ships had to deal with the new Kamikaze threat day after day, the leaders of MacArthur's Navy returned to General MacArthur's
headquarters at Lake Sentani, a spa in the Cyclops Mountains, not far from Hollandia. Admiral Kinkaid's headquarters was located on a hill near MacArthur's hill headquarters, and here the planning was done by Kinkaid, Admiral
Barbey, Admiral Wilkinson, and Admiral Oldendorf. Meanwhile, after Leyte was relatively secure, General MacArthur moved back up there, and so Admiral Kinkaid did a
good deal of shuttling back and forth in that autumn of
1944.

And finally, that autumn, with much misgiving, Admiral
Kinkaid made the decision that let the escort carriers come
into their own. It came about because the Fifth U.S. Army
Air Force could not provide the necessary close air support
for the Mindoro invasion that was needed. So after much
soul-searching, because no one really believed in the escort
carriers, Admiral Kinkaid decided that they would have to
become the primary air support for the invasion of Mindoro, and that decision was carried out. When the invasion
came on December 15, it was covered by six escort carriers,

three old battleships, three heavy cruisers, and eighteen destroyers. Admiral Halsey's Third Fleet was assigned to roam around Luzon, the planes striking the Luzon airfields and trying to prevent the build-up of Japanese air forces in the central and northern Philippines.

The Japanese were doing their best to wreck the American invasion. They had a new suicide weapon in the works, the *ohka,* or flying bomb. This was a small stub-winged plane that would be carried to its destination by a twin-engined bomber. Then the pilot of the "bomb" would go aboard, the *ohka* would be dropped loose, and it would fly on its rocket engine into—it was hoped—a carrier. The *ohka*s had been in production for several months, and the first group of them was being shipped to the Philippines aboard the new aircraft carrier *Shinano,* which was just setting out on her maiden voyage. She had fifty of these flying bombs aboard when she sailed on November 28, and passed down the coast to Kaneda Bay, along the Miura Peninsula. She was sighted by the American submarine *Archerfish* and was sunk. So down went the first contingent of flying bombs.

But there were others. On December 1, eighty-eight *ohka*s were shipped to Kure naval base for transport overseas.

On December 13, the main convoy heading for Mindoro, carrying the troops of the Twenty-fourth Infantry Division and the 503rd Parachute Infantry Regiment, was at sea on its way to invasion. Everybody, from Rear Admiral Felix B. Stump, commander of the escort carriers, on down, was expecting a real work-over by the Kamikazes.

That morning the escort carriers put up a combat air patrol of twelve fighters, and later, along came thirty-five fighters from Marine Air Group Twelve. But that morning, in Manila, Admiral Ohnishi had the word of the convoy from a Japanese reconnaissance plane, and so the newly arrived planes that had been funneled down the Japanese pipeline prepared for action. Also, from Tokyo came the orders to the two aircraft carriers *Unryu* and *Ryuho* that they were to load with planes and prepare to leave for the Philippines. Big plans were in the wind, to give the Americans yet another surprise. On December 3, Admiral Yonai, the Navy Minister, had made a trip to Kōnoike, where a new sort of air group was training. This was the Thunder-god Corps, and the planes that the men would fly were the flying bombs.

Now, as the Americans made ready for invasion, the *ohka*s were coming to the Philippines. A maintenance unit was already in place on Clark Field, and plans were made for the first *ohka* flights to originate there. On December 13, as the American invasion force was at sea, the new 27,000-ton carrier *Unryu* was ordered to load up thirty *ohka*s and sail for Manila. The *Ryuho* was ordered to take fifty-eight planes down to Taiwan. That week the navy's aerotechnical arsenal reported that it had completed 150 *ohka*s, and more were coming.

The convoy steamed along steadily toward Mindoro, that hundred-mile-long island that controlled the sea access to Luzon. The former was deep in Japanese-held territory and was important to the Allies for its air base sites. From here, the Allied forces could control the skies over Luzon when the time came for that landing.

Just before three o'clock on that afternoon of December 13, the convoy was preparing to round the southern cape of Negros Island when the Kamikazes arrived on the scene. A Japanese dive bomber carrying two bombs crashed his plane into the cruiser *Nashville*, almost as if the pilot knew that this ship was the flagship of the invasion fleet. The plane struck just behind the cabin of Admiral Struble, the invasion commander, and it virtually wiped out the command for the moment. The admiral's chief of staff was killed, as was the chief of staff of Brigadier General William C. Dunckel, the land commander. Altogether 133 officers and men were killed by this one plane, and nearly 200, including General Dunckel, were wounded. The *Nashville* was so badly damaged that Admiral Struble and the invasion staff had to transfer to a destroyer, and the *Nashville* had to go back to Leyte Gulf. Admiral Ohnishi had certainly been correct in his appraisal of the fearsome nature of the weapon he had forged.

Later that afternoon came further proof; just after 5 P.M. seven suicide planes and three escorts closed on the convoy. The American fighter planes attacked, but three Kamikazes got through the screen. Two were shot down by antiaircraft fire from the ships before they could attack, but one screamed down on the destroyer *Haraden* and crashed against the destroyer's bridge. Fourteen men were killed, twenty-four were wounded, and so much damage was done to the ship that she, too, had to return to Leyte Gulf that day.

The next day, December 14, Admiral Ohnishi planned a mass attack by nearly two hundred planes, but it miscarried. The search planes did not find the convoy that morning, but planes from Admiral Halsey's carrier fleet found the attack force as it was setting out to search, and shot down about thirty of them. The remainder staggered back to the Luzon airfields, and for the rest of the day, the overflights of American carrier planes kept the Japanese air force on the ground. A few Japanese planes from outlying bases did appear around the invasion force, but they were handled by the combat air patrol of the escort carriers and the land-based fighters that flew over the convoy in the daylight hours.

On December 15, MacArthur's Navy delivered the troops to Mindoro Island. The escort carriers peeled off then and headed back toward Leyte, for the invasion could now be covered by land-based aircraft from Leyte. But the carrier force was the target of Admiral Ohnishi's boys this day. At eight o'clock in the morning the attacks began. A Kamikaze came in out of the sun and was shot down. But another followed it and attacked the destroyer *Ralph Tal-*

bot. The destroyer's gunners shot the plane out of the sky, but the flaming wreckage hit the ship and did some damage. Admiral Ohnishi had counseled his fliers to come in low to avoid much of the antiaircraft fire, and two planes headed for the carrier *Marcus Island*. Both missed the ship and crashed in the sea, although one of the planes came so close that a wing tip decapitated a ship's lookout. Then three more Kamikazes approached the carrier *Savo Island*, but all were shot down.

Nor were all the suicide planes sent against the carriers. About twenty of them attacked the ships off the beach that were unloading the invasion troops and supplies. One struck *LST-738*, which was loaded with troops. She had to be abandoned and sunk. *LST-472* was attacked by four Kamikazes and shot down three of them, but the fourth hit and set the ship afire, so that she had to be abandoned. That ship carried much of the equipment for the construction of a PT boat base, and all that equipment was lost.

But the invasion itself was a success, and by midmorning on invasion day General Dunckel was ashore, and the control passed into the hands of the army. By nightfall the ships had been unloaded, and Admiral Struble was ready to go back to Leyte.

During the next few days the suicide planes continued to attack the beach, but there really were no adequate targets for them, so it was effort wasted. The engineers wasted very little time in building the airstrips, and soon fighters were using the Mindoro air bases.

Still the Kamikazes continued to arrive. On December 19 the first resupply convoy came in and was promptly attacked. *LST-460*, *LST-749*, and the cargo ship *Juan de Fuca* were all damaged by suicide pilots, and the two LSTs were sunk.

Meanwhile the *Unryu* sailed from Sasebo for Manila with her flying bombs aboard, and in Tokyo the Imperial Navy announced the merging of the Thundergod Corps and the T-Special Attack Corps, which had been formed on Taiwan to sink American carriers. The new organization would be called the Eleventh Air Unit. Three of its four divisions were dispatched to the Philippines. But when they arrived, they were disappointed. The *Unryu,* sailing south toward Formosa Strait, was spotted by the American submarine *Redfish,* which, on December 19, in the East China Sea, sank her with all her *ohka*s aboard.

The Mindoro landings had aroused the Japanese, and the Imperial General Headquarters sent Rear Admiral Masanori Kimura with a squadron to wipe them out. The admiral sailed in the destroyer *Kami,* with the heavy cruiser *Ashigara* and the light cruiser *Oyodo* and five more destroyers, to shell the Mindoro beachhead and sink any ships he saw.

American planes spotted the Japanese force as it neared Mindoro, but there was nothing to stop them. The battleships and the escort carriers had long gone back to Leyte Gulf. Admiral Kinkaid did send up some flying boats, and the land-based air force on Leyte was alerted. Admiral Kinkaid also started off a relieving task force of fourteen ships under Rear Admiral Theodore E. Chandler, but it was a long, long way off on the night of December 26, 1944, when Admiral Kimura attacked. All that Admiral Kinkaid could do that night was rely on his PT boats for protection of the bridgehead.

The Japanese came down, shelled the beachhead, and did some damage. The PT boats attacked but to no avail. The Allied aircraft attacked and did not do any damage, either, until that next morning when *PT-223* saw a Japanese destroyer, fired two torpedoes, and sank the 2,100-ton *Kiyoshimo.* Allied planes then continued to attack, and in the end most of the Japanese ships were hit, although only the one Japanese destroyer was sunk.

The Kimura raid was bad for American morale on Mindoro, because it started the rumor that the Japanese had made a counterlanding, but the actual damage done was very slight. The Japanese navy really did not have the power, any more, to make a serious impact on the invasion forces, except from the air, where the Kamikazes operated. But even in this area the Japanese faced great difficulty now that the Americans controlled the skies over the Philippines. The new *Ryuho* had delivered its *ohka*s safely to Taiwan. But how were they to be gotten to the Philippines for operations? It was fourteen hundred kilometers from Takeo, the southernmost Japanese air base in Taiwan, to the Philippines. The twin-engined bombers, which were to carry the *ohka*s, could hardly make the trip and return, but they might do so. Still, the bombers had to be protected en route by fighters, and the fighters could not make the trip, so they had to be staged to the Philippines beforehand.

To resolve all these knotty problems, Vice-Admiral Ryunosuke Kusaka was sent to Clark Field to work with Admiral Ohnishi to devise a plan for the use of the Thundergod Corps.

They decided to take the bomb out of the nose of the *ohka*. That way the twin-engined bomber could make the flight to Clark Field, where the 1,200-kilogram bombs would be restored or replaced. But as was so often the case these days, everything had to be delayed, and so the *ohka* attacks were postponed until mid-January, and the pilots and ground crews waited.

As it turned out, they waited in vain. Events moved so rapidly in December and January that before the *ohka*-bearing twin-engined bombers could be dispatched, the whole Japanese naval air operation in the Philippines came to an end, and the pilots and the ground crew members who had reached the Clark Field area were stranded. The *ohka* was never used in the Philippines campaign.

Following Admiral Kimura's raid on the Mindoro landing bases, Admiral Kinkaid was careful to assign more protection to the area. Admiral Chandler's cruiser force came up on December 27 to protect the area against any more

Japanese incursions. That arrival brought forth another furious set of Kamikaze attacks.

On December 28 a new supply convoy came up to Mindoro. That morning half a dozen suicide planes from Cebu attacked the new convoy. One plane dived into the cargo ship *John Burke*. That ship was loaded with ammunition for the Mindoro forces, and it exploded with a roar. When the smoke died down, there was nothing on the water where the *John Burke* had been. Another suicide plane hit the cargo ship *William Sharon* and set her afire, but the fires were put out and the ship was towed back to Leyte. Later that day the *LST-750* was also sunk by a suicide plane. On December 29 the Kamikazes attacked in force once again and hit the tender *Orestes,* which had to be beached. Another hit the destroyer *Pringle,* and another the destroyer *Gansevoort,* and another the tanker *Porcupine,* and still another the Liberty ship *Hobart Baker.*

Nearly every day at least one ship was hit. On December 31 the *Juan de Fuca* was hit again and had to be grounded. So was the *Simeon G. Reed* attacked that day and also grounded. The furious attacks on the Mindoro forces continued right up until the day that the Americans invaded Lingayen Gulf, and Admiral Ohnishi and his army counterpart turned their attention northward. In the first thirty days of occupation of Mindoro the Americans counted 334 separate air raids, most of them by suicide pilots.

The Kamikazes were the most serious weapon that MacArthur's Navy had to face, and as the Allies moved northward, they could rest assured that the situation was going to grow more serious, not less.

22

LINGAYEN

For the Japanese in the Philippines, the New Year 1945 marked the beginning of the end. Admiral Ohnishi and Admiral Fukudome had just about run out of aircraft to man the Kamikaze missions. The planes were still coming off the production lines in Japan, but as the fighting situation worsened for the Japanese on Leyte and Mindoro islands, the Imperial General Headquarters became ever more reluctant to commit planes to the Philippines operations. The plans had changed. The new great battle would be fought on the shores of Japan, the high command had decided. All resources must now be assembled for that struggle.

How times had changed for the Americans. A year earlier Admiral Kinkaid had scrimped and finagled in order to mount his amphibious operations. But at the end of 1944, with the American drive moving fast toward the heart of Germany (in spite of the temporary setback of the German Ardennes offensive of Christmas, 1944), there was plenty of everything that had been in short supply before; LSTs, amphibious tractors (LVTs), ships, and men. New faces had joined MacArthur's Navy for the coming operations.

One of these was Rear Admiral Ingolf N. Kiland, who came from Admiral King's office to sea duty. He would land one of the two forces to invade Luzon Island at Lingayen Gulf, and was bringing the men of the Thirty-seventh Infantry Division from Bougainville, along with Major General O. W. Griswold, commander of the Fourteenth Army Corps.

The second landing would be made under Rear Admiral Forrest B. Royal, who had come to the Pacific Fleet in the summer of 1944 as an amphibious commander and had now joined MacArthur's Navy. He was picking up the Fortieth Division at Cape Gloucester.

Admiral Barbey had now been fleeted up to be vice-admiral, and so had Admiral Oldendorf. Admiral Wilkinson, also now a vice-admiral, had been promoted to be chief of staff to Admiral Kinkaid.

Admiral Barbey would command the San Fabian attack force and the attack on White Beach. The force for San Fabian was built around the First Army Corps, under Major General I. P. Swift, and particularly the Forty-third Infantry Division. Rear Admiral W. M. Fechteler, under Barbey, would command the attack on Blue Beach. Admiral Wilkinson would command the attack at Lingayen. Admiral Halsey's Third Fleet would range around the islands, hitting the airfields hard. Close air support would be given by seventeen escort carriers and by hundreds of shore-based Allied aircraft from PBY patrol bombers down to fighter planes.

The first element to arrive off Luzon was Admiral Oldendorf's bombardment group, now expanded to more than a hundred and sixty ships, including six battleships, six cruisers, and the escort carriers. They came up through Surigao Strait, into the Sulu Sea, on January 3. That day the attack force was in turn attacked by a single Kamikaze, which was shot down as it tried to attack the escort carrier *Makin Island*.

But the next day, January 4, matters took a turn for the worse. Admiral Ohnishi and the Japanese army air force authorities at Clark Field had committed almost all of their remaining aircraft to stop this new invasion attempt, and that meant more than two hundred planes. On the evening of January 4, a flight of suicide planes attacked the Oldendorf force on the edge of the Sulu Sea, and a twin-engined bomber headed straight down onto the escort carrier *Ommaney Bay*, smashed into the island, cartwheeled across the flight deck, and exploded. One bomb went into the hangar deck, and another bomb penetrated the engine room, started fires, and wrecked the carrier's capacity to fight them by knocking out the water pumping system. Within the hour the torpedoes in the hangar deck began to explode, and that was the end of *Ommaney Bay*. Admiral Oldendorf ordered her sunk, and the destroyer *Burns* put a torpedo into her.

By that time the Kamikazes were giving the Oldendorf flotilla a working-over. A Kamikaze nearly missed the carrier *Lunga Point*—smashing into the sea only fifty yards away.

On January 5, Oldendorf's ships were steaming up the side of Luzon Island, just about opposite Manila and Clark Field's airstrips. Japanese search planes sighted the force, and twenty planes set out. Just before eight o'clock in the morning they approached the American ships, but the heavy combat air patrol shot down nine Japanese planes, and the others turned back to their bases. Later that morning, another formation of about twenty-five planes was also intercepted and forced away from the Oldendorf ships.

That afternoon of January 5, two Japanese destroyers, heading for Taiwan, ran afoul of the American force and were chased by destroyers and attacked by carrier planes from the escort carriers. A torpedo bomber put a torpedo into the *Momi* and sank her—another feather for the caps of the escort carrier men. Later in the afternoon, when the American ships were off Corregidor, they were attacked again by twenty planes, sixteen of them suicide planes. These were the Kikusuii (Cherry Blossom) units from

Mabalacat airfield, the cream of the crop of Admiral Ohnishi's Kamikaze Corps.

One suicide pilot dived on the cruiser *Louisville* and smashed into her. Another hit the Australian cruiser H.M.A.S. *Australia,* which on October 21 had already taken aboard one of the first of the suicide planes, with heavy casualties. Again she had fifty casualties but could continue to operate. H.M.A.S. *Arunta* was damaged by a near miss that killed two men. The escort carrier *Savo Island* had a narrow escape when one of Admiral Ohnishi's boys steered his suicide plane at the carrier and came so close that he knocked the radar antenna before splashing into the sea.

Then, two of the fighter-pilots-turned-suicide-pilots flew their Zero fighters into the escort carrier *Manila Bay*. They came in low, beneath the guns, then pulled up to 800 feet altitude and dived. The first Zero smashed into the carrier's flight deck near the island, and the bomb exploded in the hangar deck. Only quick work by the damage control parties prevented the *Manila Bay* from going the way of *Ommaney Bay*. The second Zero missed, splashing down 50 feet from the carrier.

That afternoon the destroyer escort *Stafford* was also hit by a Kamikaze, with considerable damage, and the destroyer *Helm* was hit by a suicide plane that knocked off one mast and injured half a dozen men. Another Kamikaze hit one of the minesweepers.

On January 5, Admiral Barbey's invasion ships were steaming along in the South China Sea when they also were attacked by Kamikazes and midget submarines. A midget submarine aimed two torpedoes at the cruiser *Boise*, but both missed. A Kamikaze hit the *LST-912* that day.

That night four of Barbey's destroyers reported a surface contact, went out to chase it, and sank the Japanese escort *Hinoki*, which was fleeing from Manila to Cam Ranh Bay. A Kamikaze hit the escort carrier *Kadashan Bay,* which was escorting the Barbey force, and forced the little carrier to retreat to Leyte.

By that evening, Admiral Ohnishi knew that the Americans were heading for Lingayen Gulf, and on the morning of January 6 he staged his supreme effort. He ordered his planes to go up the next day in force.

But the Allies were also on the alert. General MacArthur asked that Admiral Halsey make a special effort to pulverize the Luzon airfields on January 6, and Halsey gave the orders.

Shortly before dawn, the Oldendorf ships were rounding Cape Bolinao, at the edge of Lingayen Gulf, and were deployed to carry out their fire support missions for the invasion ships that were coming along behind them.

The minesweepers were beginning to work at first light, when a dozen enemy planes approached, but the combat air patrol was already up, and they intercepted and shot down five planes, losing one American fighter in the process. After that, all was quiet until after eleven o'clock in the morning, when many Kamikazes began to attack.

One brushed by the destroyer *Richard P. Leary* and crashed in the sea. The battleship *New Mexico* was hit by a suicide plane as she was bombarding the shore at San Fabian. Many people were killed, including a high-ranking British liaison officer and a war correspondent who was on the ship's bridge.

The destroyer *Walke* was attacked simultaneously by four suicide planes, and one of them hit her, causing serious damage and casualties. The destroyer *Allen M. Sumner* was also hit, with forty-three casualties, as was the destroyer *Brooks*, and the minesweeper *Long* was sunk.

The damage might have been worse that day, except that Admiral Halsey's planes appeared over those Luzon airfields and attacked time after time using three task groups. The Japanese were lucky: The air over Clark Field's complex was heavily overcast, and the American planes did not do much of a job. They destroyed only thirty-two Japanese aircraft, with a high loss of seventeen American planes that day. But they did keep some planes on the ground and thus saved Admiral Oldendorf from a worse beating than he took.

Admiral Barbey's ships were also a target again. The attack transport *Callaway* was hit by a suicide diver, which killed twenty-nine men and wounded twenty-two, but the invading troops, belowdecks, were unhurt.

The next day, January 7, Admiral Ohnishi continued his desperate effort. Not much came of it until after five o'clock that evening. The planes of Task Force Thirty-eight had been ranging around Luzon, keeping the suicide planes from taking off. But in midafternoon five suicide pilots from Mabalacat got into the air with a fighter escort-observer. They headed for Lingayen Gulf, and shortly before five-thirty they arrived. One crashed into the battleship *California*. The damage was really serious, with 200 casualties. Another suicide plane crashed into the light cruiser *Columbia* with such force that the bomb penetrated three decks before it exploded. The ship lost 57 men and was out of the fight.

H.M.A.S. *Australia* was also another target this day, and again was unlucky and took a hit that caused forty more casualties aboard. The *Louisville* was hit a second time: Rear Admiral Theodore E. Chandler, commander of the cruiser division, was killed, with eighty-seven other casualties. The ship was so badly damaged that it had to pull out of the invasion.

The destroyer *O'Brien* took a Kamikaze that day, and the destroyer-minesweeper *Southard* did, too. By the end of the day Admiral Kinkaid had a doleful count: Twenty-five American ships had been sunk or damaged by suicide planes in these four days of attack, and early the next morning, the *Hovey* was sunk, too.

That evening of January 7 the minesweeper *Palmer* was sunk by two bombs dropped by a conventional Japanese bomber. In spite of the damage they inflicted, the Kamikazes were not very active that day, for at Clark Field, Admiral Fukudome, the commander of the Second Naval Air Fleet, had ordered a withdrawal from Luzon to Taiwan. (The planes were flying, but they were not attacking.) Admiral Ohnishi was also getting ready to move out.

But there was some activity by army pilots. The *Australia,* after evading one Kamikaze that day, was hit by another that had already been shot down but skidded along the water to blow a hole fourteen feet wide in the side of the ship. Still the *Australia* continued to operate.

The invasion troops were getting ready to come in. The ships had sailed as early as the last few days of December, and they were nearing Lingayen.

On the evening of January 8, Admiral Wilkinson's Lingayen attack force came up with Admiral Barbey's force and got into position for the landings. That night, an hour before sunset, the Kamikazes started to come in again. This time six planes attacked, and one of them crashed into the *Kitkun Bay,* again damaging her, this time with a hole nine feet wide and twenty feet long, but not putting her out of action, although her speed was cut to ten knots.

No one knew quite what to expect on the morning of January 9, the day of the landings at San Fabian, but Admiral Ohnishi was just getting ready to leave for Taiwan, and Admiral Fukudome had already gone. The planes had either been shipped out or sent on their final missions, and all of the staff officers had gone. The remaining junior officers and enlisted men were forming themselves into brigades of infantry, to move into the mountains to make a last stand.

On the morning of invasion day the American fleet at Lingayen was attacked by army suicide planes. The destroyer escort *Hodges* was hit, but no one was hurt, because the plane knocked off the foremast and radio antenna, but did not make the deck, and splashed alongside the ship. The cruiser *Columbia* was hit again, with ninety-two casualties.

As for the landings, they were easy enough. There was virtually no opposition on the beaches, for General Yamashita had decided that his fight would be waged in the mountains. A few ships were hit by 75-mm shells from shore guns, but the casualties could be counted in the dozens, not the hundreds. The primary opposition, little as it was, continued to come from the air. That afternoon of the invasion day, the *Mississippi* was hit, and eighty-six men were killed or wounded. The *Australia* was clipped again, but the suicide plane hit the smokestack and fell overboard, doing little damage. It was the *Australia*'s number five "devil-diver."

By invasion day, the Japanese navy was finished in the Philippines, but the army continued to fight, and the army planes were now almost all suicide planes as well. There was a big difference: The navy fliers had been mostly fighter pilots of considerable skill, but the army pilots who had come down to the Philippines in the suicide corps were tyros. All this showed in what occurred. On the night of the landings, just before sunset, several Kamikazes approached the invasion fleet. All of them were shot down well before they threatened the ships. In fact the worst damage that night came from a new weapon, suicide boats operated by Japanese soldiers. These were eighteen-foot plywood motorboats, carrying 500 pounds of explosives. That night about seventy of them attacked the invasion fleet, and they managed to damage some ships. *LCI-974* was sunk, and eight attack transports were damaged. Four other LSTs, a transport, and an LCI were hit, but only the LCI was damaged badly enough to be abandoned.

On January 10, as Admiral Ohnishi and his staff boarded their plane for the trip to Taiwan, army Kamikazes kept hitting the ships off the beaches. Once in a while one connected, as with the destroyer escort *Le Ray Wilson,* which was seriously damaged, with thirteen casualties. But by the afternoon on that day the Lingayen airstrip was ready for action, and land-based Allied fighters could be brought in, thus reducing the danger from suicide attacks considerably.

But the suicide pilots kept coming. An army fighter plunged into the transport *Du Page,* killing and injuring 190 people. The reinforcements came up under Admiral Conolly on January 11, and their arrival occasioned a new spurt of Kamikaze attacks. Nearly all of them were shot down without making their dives. But on January 12, the destroyer escorts *Gilligan* and *Richard W. Suesens* were attacked. A Kamikaze virtually wiped up the deck of the *Gilligan,* knocking out a whole gun crew. The *Suesens* had come to the ship's aid when a Kamikaze attacked her, but the pilot was not very skillful and the plane did not hit.

The destroyer *Belknap* and the Liberty ship *Otis Skinner* were damaged in the gulf, as were more arriving ships. On January 12, four more ships were hit. The odds around the Philippines were going up for the Japanese, it seemed. On January 13, several Kamikazes attacked a slow convoy of forty-three ships west of Manila and damaged *LST-700.* But it took four Kamikazes to do it, which meant the Japanese had lost four planes and four pilots to damage only one American LST.

The last attack that produced results for the Japanese was made against the escort carrier *Salamaua.* The plane plunged through the flight deck and delivered 500 pounds of explosives. The carrier was not badly damaged, however, and continued to operate.

After that there were no more attacks, because there were virtually no more Japanese aircraft left on the island of Luzon. So by January 18, the American forces were ashore and well established on the island of Luzon, and General MacArthur was looking forward to recapturing Manila. Admiral Kinkaid's Seventh Fleet—MacArthur's Navy—now had the job of policing the Mindoro-Lingayen sea lanes, to be sure the transports could continue to bring the supplies and men that would be needed to fight General Yamashita's powerful forces on Luzon.

23

CLEANUP

After the Lingayen landings, General MacArthur hoped to capture Manila in about two weeks, but his hopes were dashed by a series of adverse circumstances.

First, the Japanese slowed the army by a series of delaying actions: blowing up bridges, destroying the roads, and tearing up the tracks of the railroads. By the end of January, the Americans had reached the Clark Field complex north of Manila, but they had not captured the capital. On January 29 MacArthur's Navy landed the Eleventh Corps about forty-five miles from San Fernando, thus sealing off the Bataan Peninsula and preventing the Japanese from doing there what the Americans had done in 1942, staging a long, last-ditch stand.

Admiral Struble commanded the landing forces until they were established ashore. He landed 30,000 troops on invasion day. He used transports, Liberty ships, and LSTs. They were protected by a light cruiser and a number of destroyers and the escort carriers, which by now had become routinely accepted as the first line of air defense in landings.

The opposition was very light, because General Yamashita had decided to hole up in the mountains around Baguio, and there to conduct his last-ditch defenses of the Philippines. In fact, Admiral Struble did not even need a bombardment, because there were fewer than fifty Japanese in the area. So the bombardment was canceled, and the troops swarmed ashore and were greeted enthusiastically by the Filipinos, who were waving flags and shouting for freedom. The one real act of war violence was the torpedoing of the transport *Cavalier* off Grande Island on January 31, by a Japanese submarine.

On January 31, also, Admiral Fechteler's ships landed the Eleventh Airborne Division, which was to march toward Manila from the Nasugbu side on the west. Again there was no opposition, and the troops landed and reached the Pasig River before the end of the day.

There were Japanese troops around here, however, and when night fell, out came the suicide boats, which had been concealed along the shore. One of them blew a hole in *PC-1129* and sank her, but only one member of the crew was lost. The destroyer escort *Lough* found about twenty-five small boats and fired on them with her small guns. The destroyer *Claxton* did the same. The boats fired a few torpedoes, all of which missed, and then retired, because they could not break through to attack the transports as had been their intention. The worst problem offered by the Japanese midgets hereabouts was the confusion between them and American PT boats, and as a consequence *PT-77* and *PT-79* were sunk by American destroyers when the recognition signals got mixed up.

By early February the Bataan Peninsula was sealed off, just about as it had been by the Japanese in the early weeks of 1942. General MacArthur then ordered amphibious landings on Corregidor and in the Mariveles area. Admiral Barbey called on Admiral Struble to lead the assault, and Struble loaded up the 151st Regimental Combat Team. The troops were brought up from Subic Bay, and then the 503rd Parachute Infantry Regiment was airdropped on Corregidor. Once again it was a case of a large force being employed against a small remnant of Japanese, for there were not even fifteen hundred enemy troops in the whole area, except on Corregidor, where there were about five thousand naval sailors, now fighting as infantry. In fact, the Japanese navy was the main force that the Americans faced in this area. General Yamashita had planned to evacuate Manila (as the Americans had done in 1942) and to leave the central Luzon plain to the Americans. But Vice-Admiral Denshichi Okochi, the navy area commander, had other ideas. He set up a separate naval defense force, and that force chose to fight for the streets of Manila. There were about sixteen thousand sailors involved, and they fought all the way. The local commander, Rear Admiral Sanji Iwabachi, defended Manila to the bitter end. In a month of fighting, his twenty thousand troops were wiped out in house-to-house fighting, and, unfortunately for history, culture, and architecture buffs, so was the old Spanish City of Manila.

The Japanese dug in on Corregidor, where the navy also made a stout defense, using guns in caves and from various strong points to fire on the American ships. Admiral Berkey's covering force of cruisers and destroyers returned the fire and knocked out the cave guns one by one. The destroyer *Fletcher* was hit by gunfire; so was the destroyer *Hopewell,* hard enough to be sent back to Manus for repairs; and so was the minesweeper *YMS-48,* which was set afire. Two destroyers, the *La Vallette* and the *Radford,* were damaged by mines when they were trying to sink floaters. They were part of the minesweeping unit of MacArthur's Navy, and they were in a hurry to clear up Manila Bay for logistical reasons that extended throughout the Pacific.

On February 15 extensive minesweeping was finished, Corregidor was under fire by various ships, and an air strike came in. The troops landed on the beach at Mariveles Harbor at 10 A.M., and the only serious problem was a loose mine that damaged the *LSM-169.*

The Japanese holed up in their caves and fought hard for ten days. The destroyers stood off the beaches and delivered fire to help the troops. When it was over, about forty-five hundred dead Japanese were counted, and it was estimated that another five hundred had been sealed up in caves. The Americans suffered about eight hundred fifty casualties, almost a third of them injured in the parachute airdrops.

In February the ships and men of MacArthur's Navy were busy with the army, clearing up the islands of Manila Bay. Caballo, El Fraile, Carabao Island, all were taken. For two months the navy then worked to clear Manila Harbor of sunken wrecks and mines. By the middle of March Manila was relatively safe for shipping, although several ships did strike mines after that time.

The last gasp in the cleanup of the Manila area was an amphibious landing on the Bicol Peninsula near the southern tip of Luzon. The purpose was to clear the San Bernardino Strait and thus shorten the passage from the south to Manila. The Japanese had established a significant garrison in the area to watch the strait, although the reason for it had now evaporated, since the Japanese no longer had any significant naval forces in the islands.

Admiral Barbey sent Captain Homer F. McGee to command the amphibious expedition. The 158th Regimental Combat Team was taken, largely by landing craft infantry (LCIs), to Legaspi and landed on April 1, 1945. There was no sea, no air, and no land opposition. The main Japanese contingent consisted of a single battery of guns, a handful of snipers, and one roadblock five hundred yards from the shore. Once that was wiped out, only a few snipers remained, and the Bicol Peninsula was soon cleared.

MacArthur's Navy then lost most of its transports, which had to be taken back to Pearl Harbor and made ready for the Iwo Jima and Okinawa operations. But they were no longer needed. The army had its own transports, and the navy had its fire support ships, and landing ships and craft. In the next few months Admiral Barbey would be very busy, planning and conducting thirty-two troop movements, mostly to clear up isolated pockets of Japanese troops. The plans were being made for the most important of these strategies, a landing at Palawan and one at Zamboanga to clear important areas.

The war was far from over. General Yamashita still had about one hundred seventy-five thousand troops on Luzon Island. But the amphibious phase of the operations in the Philippines was coming to its end.

24

WAR IN THE SOUTH

With the liberation of Manila early in 1945, the world considered the war in the Philippines to be about at an end. The truth was quite different, for Yamashita was determined to hold out as long as he could, and in the south there were many strong points that had to be dealt with in a war that had lost the glamour of chanciness and was now reduced to the slogging danger of attrition.

General MacArthur then continued to employ his navy to clean up the Philippines and planned also to capture Borneo and the Dutch East Indies, which he would hand back to the Dutch government, thus restoring the status quo antebellum. He did not consult the people of the East Indies or anyone else.

The Joint Chiefs of Staff had many other things on their minds, and they let MacArthur have his head as long as he could operate with his own forces at hand and did not ask for anything from them. So the cleanup of the area continued. Lieutenant General Robert L. Eichelberger, who had been with MacArthur since the days of Papua, was the land commander. Admiral Kinkaid was the commander of MacArthur's Navy still. And they combined forces to do MacArthur's bidding.

Early in February 1945, Admiral Kinkaid moved his headquarters to Tolsa, in Leyte Gulf, and there began to plan for a series of mop-up operations. Admiral Barbey was back in his headquarters aboard the command ship *Blue Ridge*, which moved around from one bay to another as seemed necessary. Except for the occasional Japanese submarine foray, and they were no more than that, the waters around the Philippines had been turned into a group of American lakes. Admiral Barbey could steam more or less where he pleased in comparative safety.

After the capture of Manila, the air forces wanted bases in Palawan, which is a hundred and fifty miles closer to the Indochina Peninsula than any bases the air force then had. So MacArthur was happy to oblige and take Palawan.

There were about three thousand Japanese troops on Palawan Island, so the army chose to use the 186th Regimental Combat Team, with about six thousand fighting troops, to make the assault. Admiral Fechteler was responsible for the landing, which came on February 28, 1945. The initial bombardment of the landing beaches at Puerto Princesa was carried out by the cruisers *Denver, Montpelier,* and *Cleveland,* and four destroyers. General Eichelberger flew over the beachhead in a B-17 and watched the landings. The scene was satisfying, but not exciting. There was no opposition, except for scattered small-arms fire. The Japanese had pulled back into the hills, where they did fight to the end. For the infantry it was the arduous process of routing them out, cave by cave, machine gun by machine gun, but for the navy the job was finished, and the building of the airfields could proceed.

The next step MacArthur wanted was the capture of Zamboanga on Mindanao Island. This was going to be a tougher nut to crack, because there were some eight thousand Japanese troops there. Admiral Royal was designated as commander of the expedition. The plans were made, and they proceeded very well. The invasion was made on March 10 without incident—the only noise being the sound of the Japanese blowing up the jetty in the town of Zamboanga.

The day before, a B-24 bomber had exploded in midair, and for a while there was concern about Japanese super-weapons, but the fact was that the bomber had been hit by a bomb from another B-24.

On invasion day a single Japanese battery fired on the ships as the troops were coming ashore and hit two landing craft infantry (LCIs). The cruisers and the destroyers fired on the beaches. One LST was damaged by a round from a Japanese mortar, but by nightfall of invasion day the beachhead had moved inland a mile and a half. Thereafter the Japanese artillery gave some trouble, but the cruiser *Boise* took care of that, using a spotter plane and finding and destroying the guns. Only on March 12 did any serious opposition begin.

That opposition began near Pasanaca, in the foothills of the mountains. The next twelve days saw heavy fighting and the use of cruisers and destroyers to fire on special targets. On March 24 it was all over, and southern Mindanao had been secured.

Next came Panay, Cebu, Negros, and Bohol. The Japanese had some fifty thousand troops on these islands, and General MacArthur wanted them eliminated. Admiral Struble was chosen to land the Fortieth Division on Panay, and he did so on March 16. The troops ran into no serious opposition on the beaches. There was no problem at sea, and there were no Kamikazes flying in the air. The Japanese defended the cities for a little while but then moved back into the hills. It was a very much simpler war than the Americans had fought in the earlier days.

On March 20, Iloilo, the capital of Panay, was captured. Then came the seizure of Negros Occidental on March 29. It was another easy landing, made easier by the fact that American-oriented guerrillas controlled two-thirds of the island, although there were some fifteen thousand Japanese troops there. Again the Japanese fought and then withdrew into the mountains. Again it was an easy bit of war.

On March 26 the Allies attacked Cebu. These landings were so easy that the old pros let their assistants do the work. Admiral Barbey delegated the Cebu landing to Captain Albert T. Sprague, his chief of staff. Since there were so many experienced amphibious men now, and so little enemy opposition, Admiral Fechteler was moved up to Washington to take a promotion and a desk job. The war seemed to be grinding to a stop, except for the specter of the future, caused by that Japanese determination to fight to the bitter end, which would have to come somewhere in the mountains of Hokkaidō.

General Yamashita had ordained the new Japanese defense posture in the Philippines, which was to let the Allies make their landings, since these could not be safely contested anyhow, and then to withdraw, creating as much trouble as possible with as little loss as possible, and hole up in the mountains to make the enemy come after them. Occasionally, however, some local commander changed the rules, and it was thus on Cebu.

For a change, the Japanese elected to fight at Cebu on the beaches. Some twelve thousand Japanese troops were concentrated in and around Cebu City. They had established strong defensive positions in the past five months since the landings on Leyte.

The bombardment force plastered the beaches for an hour and a half, and then the troops of the American division landed. But here they encountered land mines, and that meant the engineers had to go out first to find the mines, remove them, mark them if they could not, and thus warn the troops about the dangers. The destroyers chased and finally sank a midget submarine. That was the extent of the naval opposition.

At the beginning of April the clearing of Bohol and Negros Oriental began. Again it was accomplished by the use of landing craft and LCMs. The distances were short, and besides, MacArthur's Navy had been stripped of most of its big cargo and transport ships because of the needs of the Pacific Fleet. Again the guerrillas had much of the area under control, so the going was relatively easy for the 164th Infantry Regiment. So the southern Visayas were liberated. What remained now was Mindanao proper, where about forty-five thousand Japanese troops remained.

General Eichelberger decided to establish the beachhead on the western part of the island, where there were few Japanese, and then move inland. Admiral A. G. Noble commanded the amphibious operation for Admiral Barbey, and the army's Tenth Corps was to do the fighting on land. The troops went ashore near the Mindanao River. On April 22 the Americans also landed at Parang and Cotabato. The only trouble at sea came from suicide craft—one broke through the cordon of destroyers and escorts in Taloma Bay, south of Davao, on May 1. It sank a small army freighter. And, wonder of wonders these days, a single Japanese plane, coming from no one knew where, attacked the PT boats of Squadron Twenty-four in Davao Gulf.

On May 14, *PT-135* and *PT-343* discovered a concealed channel inland at Piso Point, across from Davao, and following it, they found six Japanese suicide boats in a concealed haven. Using 40-mm guns, they strafed the area, blew up one boat and then the fuel and ammunition dump, and thus destroyed another boat. They strafed all the others and withdrew. The next day a destroyer escort, the U.S.S. *Key*, came up to help them, and together they worked over the area and finished the job of destroying the Japanese base. For the rest of the month MacArthur's Navy was busy, destroying Japanese outposts and island bases, and carrying troops to clean up one area after another.

The final task for MacArthur's Navy between February and August 1945, was the occupation of Borneo, which had been the major Japanese fuel supplier during the war.

Originally it had been believed that the British would take over this operation as soon as they were freed from the war in Europe, but the British decided that it was more important for them to use their naval forces in the Pacific as part of the general strike against Japan, so General MacArthur's Navy was chosen to conduct the invasion of Borneo.

The first invasion came at Tarakan on May 1. The real problem here was not the Japanese but the mines. They had been laid by the British and Dutch during 1942, by the Japanese, and by the Allies in airdrops during the last three years of war. So much attention given to the waters off Tarakan was justified by its value as an oil center. Admiral Royal was to land the troops of the Australian Ninth Division, a part of Australia's First Corps under Lieutenant General Sir Leslie Morehead. The mines were swept by the Australians and Americans, Admiral Berkey's bombardment ships arrived, and the landings were on.

One ship hit a mine and was severely damaged. She was the destroyer *Jenkins*. The bombardment began at about 7 A.M. and lasted for an hour. The Japanese used mortars and artillery, but there was no air or sea opposition; the Japanese had virtually nothing left with which to fight except on the land. The damage to seagoing craft came from the enemy's artillery, which sank a minesweeper, *YMS-481*, and hit two others. Two Japanese 75-mm guns, well concealed, kept firing on the channel until they were finally silenced three weeks later by the destroyer escort *Douglas A. Munro*. The Australians moved in quickly and thoroughly. The H.M.A.S. *Baroo* and the destroyer escort *Formoe* stayed on call, giving fire to support the troops when they needed it, and the Australians pushed the Japanese into a small area in the mountains, where they remained until the surrender in August.

The second target on Borneo was Brunei Bay, and again Admiral Royal was the commander of the attack. On June 10, as at Mindanao, the ships coming in were attacked by a single Japanese bomber, coming again from some overlooked little base. The plane came in, dropped a single bomb, which missed, and then somehow made its way through an enormous volume of antiaircraft fire to escape unhurt. And where it went, nobody knew.

The Brunei occupation was accomplished with very little opposition. By the end of the first day it was entirely under control. The naval action of the area was confined to PT boat operations, and the boats spent their time chasing schooners and destroying Japanese barges. On June 12 that bomber came back, a Kawasaki army fighter bomber, and dropped two bombs, which again missed the ships in the harbor. And then on June 14, three planes attacked, but one was shot down and none did any damage. The Japanese army air force had reached the bottom of the barrel. The pilots who flew the planes were scarcely able to manage their aircraft.

The third Borneo landing was made at Balikpapan, the oil center of the area, across Makassar Strait from Celebes. A hundred times American submarines of MacArthur's Navy had come up that passage, seeking game in the harsher and more active days of the war. This was the last amphibious operation of MacArthur's Navy, and it went off with a bang. The prelanding bombardment lasted sixteen days.

July 1 was the date of the landing, and Admiral Noble was the commander. The troops were those of the Australian Seventh Division.

Balikpapan was heavily defended by antiaircraft guns, and so, intensive air strikes were made to knock these out. But again the problem was mines, dropped mostly by the Allies to sink Japanese tankers calling in port. On June 18 a minesweeper, *YMS-50*, blew herself up on a mine. Later three more small minesweepers were blown up by mines.

Then underwater demolition teams came in to remove the beach obstacles put up by the Japanese, finishing on June 25. It was at this point that the Japanese made their final air forays into the area, and snoopers began coming in, too, dropping bombs. Admiral Kinkaid sent down three escort carriers, the *Suwannee,* the *Chenango,* and the *Gilbert Islands.* And on July 1 the invasion came off like clockwork. Just before the landings, someone counted up the effect of bombardment: 3,000 tons of bombs, 38,000 rounds of shells, 114,000 rounds from automatic weapons, and 7,000 rockets were fired at the beach. About five hundred Japanese soldiers were killed thus. By nightfall of July 1 the beachhead was secure, and General MacArthur came down to have a look. Soon, the American contingent was pulling out, leaving the whole occupation to the Australians. The last American ship of MacArthur's Navy to leave the Balikpapan area was the destroyer *Saufley* on July 19.

General MacArthur had wanted to continue the operations in the Dutch East Indies, but the Joint Chiefs of Staff that summer decided that all efforts had to go to the coming plans for the invasion of Japan proper, so he was turned down. MacArthur's Navy, therefore, by the middle of July, had nothing more to do, and it waited out the last few days of the war as preparations were being made for Admiral Kinkaid to join in on the assault of the Japanese beaches. But it never happened, for on August 15, Emperor Hirohito decided that enough was enough and that he would not preside over the suicide of the Japanese people, and he announced the surrender of Japan. Thus World War II came to an end, the ships of the U.S. Seventh Fleet went to Japan or back to America, and in the postwar reorganization of the navy, MacArthur's Navy ceased to be.

NOTES

All of my books about the Pacific War have been dependent, to a large extent, on research materials gained from the Operational Archives of the U.S. Naval History Center in Washington D.C., and *MacArthur's Navy* is no exception. I am ever indebted to Dr. Dean Allard and his staff there.

The research for this book also included a number of interviews and discussions, especially with Vice-Admiral Daniel E. Barbey, the chief of MacArthur's Navy's Amphibious Command, Admiral Thomas C. Kinkaid, commander of MacArthur's Navy (U.S. Seventh Fleet), Rear Admiral James Fife, who commanded the fleet's submarines at Brisbane at one time, and Vice-Admiral Ralph W. Christie, who commanded the whole submarine force at one point. Also I discussed the campaigns with several correspondents who covered them, including Richard W. Johnston, then of United Press Associations, Robert Miller, also of U.P., and George Weller of the *Chicago Daily News*.

---

1. Sad Beginnings

This chapter depends largely on materials I had gathered for my book *The Lonely Ships*, the story of the American Asiatic Fleet, which was dispersed in 1942, and on interviews with Admiral Christie and Admiral Fife.

—————————2. CHANGE OF COMMAND—————

This chapter depends heavily on research materials gathered for my book *The Jungles of New Guinea,* and on several interviews with Admiral Barbey. Also the material about the problems of the far-flung submarine commands comes from correspondence and interviews with members of the crew of the U.S.S. *Bowfin,* Admiral Christie, and Admiral Fife.

—————————3. LANDINGS ON NEW BRITAIN—————

As long as Admiral Carpender remained in command of the Seventh Fleet, operations were conducted on an extremely conservative basis. He would not risk his destroyers in the waters around New Guinea, a fact that caused hardship for the troops fighting in Papua. The fact was, however, that the situation was not entirely within Admiral Carpender's control. The naval resources in the Pacific were very slender in 1942 and 1943, and Admiral Nimitz was not eager to build up General MacArthur's command in any way. Admiral Carpender's recall to other duty and the coming of Admiral Kinkaid coincided with a change in high command policy in the South Pacific, and then the Seventh Fleet really got moving. The material for the discussion of Japanese activity comes largely from the volumes of the official Japanese war history that cover the New Guinea campaign.

—————————4. CAPE GLOUCESTER—————

The Cape Gloucester campaign turned out to be almost entirely unnecessary, because the tide of war was ebbing for the Japanese and surging for the Americans so rapidly that the airfields at Cape Gloucester were really not necessary for an Allied advance. But the battles were battles, nonetheless, and men fought and died in them. The quotations in this chapter come from *The History of United States Marine Corps Operations in World War II: Isolation of Rabaul.*

—————————5. VICTORY IN THE SOUTH PACIFIC—————

The story of Admiral Kinkaid's planning comes from an interview with him. He had a very comfortable relationship with General MacArthur.

The material about the submarine command comes from my studies for my book *Bowfin,* and from interviews with Admiral Christie.

───────────────6. PRELUDE TO HOLLANDIA───────────

The Pacific campaign moved very rapidly in the summer of 1944, and the capture of the Marianas made the air war something new. But at the same time the U.S. Navy was expanding, and after the invasion at Normandy, the battle in Europe became largely a land contest, which freed most of the navy's resources for the Pacific theater. This showed itself immediately in the building of MacArthur's Navy.

───────────────7. LANDINGS IN HOLLANDIA───────────

The landings in Hollandia, the most complex yet undertaken by MacArthur's Navy, had their difficulties, most of them caused by the lack of information about the geography of this part of the world. Fortunately the Japanese were not in the area in great force, as it turned out. The blowing up of the ammunition dump was one of the expensive tragedies of the Southwest Pacific campaign.

───────────────8. TO THE VOGELKOP───────────

Perhaps the most important aspect of the Wakde campaign was the skillful use to which the Allies put the escort carriers, still a virtually unknown and unsung part of the navy. By necessity—since they did not have access to the large fleet carriers and light carriers—MacArthur's Navy made do with the escorts, and they did very well. For the submarines, life was becoming tougher as the Japanese antisubmarine defenses strengthened, and several submarines were lost. I gathered the information for this aspect from Admirals Christie and Fife.

───────────────9. SURPRISE AT BIAK───────────

The fighting grew more intense for MacArthur's Navy with the Biak campaign. And there was a portent of things to come when a plane, hit by antiaircraft fire, crashed into the subchaser *SC-99.*

————————10. A Foray of the Combined Fleet————————

The beginning of the suicide diving tactic actually antedated the coming of the Kamikazes, as this chapter shows. For many months the frustrated pilots of the Japanese naval air forces, in particular, had been advocating this tactic as the only way to slow down the American advance.

————————————11. Numfoor————————————

The Numfoor landings represented the desire of General MacArthur for more and more airfields, as he prepared to return to the Philippines. And he got them at Numfoor and Sansapoor.

————————————12. The Focus Changes————————————

The New Guinea campaign was over, and General MacArthur now played his trumps: At a meeting in Pearl Harbor he managed to convince President Franklin Roosevelt that the strategy of the Pacific campaign should be changed and that the Philippines, and not China or Taiwan, should be the next target. That put MacArthur in the driver's seat, where he had always wished to be.

As noted, the impetus for the suicide missions of the Japanese was increasing daily, as the war situation worsened for them. After the Morotai landings the Japanese knew that the next point would be somewhere in the Philippines.

————————————13. The Leyte Plan————————————

The planning for Leyte brought from the Japanese the strongest reaction of the last two years, in the decision to pit the entire remnants of the Japanese fleet in one last desperate gamble to stop the progress of the Americans. But the Japanese did not really understand just how much might the Americans could now assemble, with the betterment of fortunes in Europe. The Seventh Fleet, MacArthur's Navy, was more powerful in 1944 than the whole Pacific Fleet had been in 1941. All that was lacking were fleet carriers, and this shortage was met by the many escort carriers available to the fleet.

Notes

---------------------14. LEYTE: BEGINNINGS---------------------

The story about the invasion of Leyte comes largely from research done for my book *The Battle of Leyte Gulf*. The Japanese side comes from the Japanese defense agency's official history of the war, and from the biography of General Yamashita and the biography of Admiral Ohnishi.

---------------------15. LANDINGS ON LEYTE---------------------

The story of Admiral Halsey's Third Fleet comes largely from my Leyte book and from my *McCampbell's Heroes*, the story of the air fighters of the carrier *Essex*. The story of the escort carriers' combat comes from *The Men of the Gambier Bay*.

---------------------16. REACTION---------------------

The story of the Kamikazes comes from my *The Kamikazes*, and from the biography of Admiral Ohnishi and the diary of Admiral Ugaki.

---------------------17. ACTION AT SURIGAO STRAIT---------------------

The story of the *Dace* and the *Darter* comes from my *Submarines at War*. The account of the battle of Surigao Strait is from my *The Battle of Leyte Gulf*. The story of the Japanese countereffort is from the Japanese Self Defense Agency history. Also I used Samuel Eliot Morison's volume on Leyte, from his massive *History of United States Naval Operations in World War II*.

---------------------18. ONE DOWN, TWO TO GO---------------------

The story of the American pursuit of the straggling Japanese forces is told from Morison's account and from my own Leyte book. The air activity of the Japanese comes from *The Kamikazes* and from *McCampbell's Heroes*.

---------------------19. THE BATTLE OFF SAMAR---------------------

The story of the brave battle of the escort carriers comes from my research for *The Men of the Gambier Bay* and the Leyte book. The "jeep" carriers did a magnificent job of routing Admiral Kurita's vastly superior surface force, thus proving once again that the era of the battleship really ended with World War I. The gallant fight of the destroyers and escorts comes from Morison and from my own *Gambier Bay* book.

20. KAMIKAZE!

The tales of the Kamikazes come from the biography of Admiral Ohnishi and the Kamikaze book. The story of the attacks on the escort carriers comes from Morison. The stories of the later landings come from Morison and from the Yamashita biography.

21. TO LUZON

The story of the *ohka* and other tales from Japan are from the Japanese self-defense agency series and from the Ohnishi biography.

22. LINGAYEN

With the Lingayen landings, the Seventh Fleet had very nearly finished its job. The fleet was now a major element of the American navy and was virtually self-contained. With the capture of many airfields in the Philippines, there was no longer need for carriers in this part of the world. The difficulties of carriers in the face of the Japanese suicide attacks is very well shown in the stories, most of which come from the works on the suicide planes. Morison was also very useful in setting the stage for the American activity.

23. CLEANUP

After Lingayen, the story of the Seventh Fleet really became anticlimactic. The activity more or less consisted of a "cleanup" of the Philippines, necessary but not exciting. Corregidor Island, the Bicol Peninsula, and the occupation of Negros and other southern islands all came apace. Morison's volume was invaluable here.

Notes

24. WAR IN THE SOUTH

So the victories continued, Zamboanga, Panay, Cebu, Bohol, all essential, but not very exciting. The Seventh Fleet was like a three-ring circus, something going all the time, somebody juggling here, there, and everywhere. And finally came the occupation of Borneo, which wiped out the Japanese petroleum resources in the East Indies—and brought the war around full circle, for it had been those petroleum resources that had caused the Japanese to start the Pacific War in the first place.

BIBLIOGRAPHY

Boei Cho Bogyo Kenshujo Senshi Shitsu Cho, Boston: Atlantic Little Brown, 1950–56. The 101-volume official Japanese history of World War II.

Ebina, Kashiko. *Saigo no Tokko Ki (The Last Suicide Plane).* Tokyo: Yamashita Mitsuo Tosho Shuppangaisha, 1975. A biography of Vice-Admiral Matome Ugaki.

Hoyt, Edwin P. *The Battle of Leyte Gulf.* New York: Weybright and Talley, 1972.

————*Bowfin.* New York: Van Nostrand Reinhold, 1980.

————*Japan's War.* New York: McGraw-Hill, 1986.

————*The Jungles of New Guinea.* New York: Avon Books, 1988.

————*The Kamikazes.* New York: Arbor House, 1980.

————*McCampbell's Heroes.* New York: Van Nostrand Reinhold, 1979.

————*The Men of the Gambier Bay.* Middleboro: Paul Eriksson, 1979.

————*Submarines at War*. New York: Stein and Day, 1983.

Kusanayagi, Daizo. *Tokko no Shizo (The Kamikaze Idea)*. Tokyo: Bungei Haru Aki, 1972. A biography of Admiral Takejiro Ohnishi.

Millot, Bernard. *Divine Thunder*. New York: Pinnacle Books, 1972.

Morison, Samuel Eliot. *History of United States Naval Operations in World War II*. Vols. 6, 8, 12, 13, 14. Boston: Atlantic Little Brown, 1950–1956.

Shaw, Henry I., Jr., and Major Douglas T. Kane. *The History of United States Marine Corps Operations in World War II. Isolation of Rabaul,* vol 2. Washington, D.C.: U.S. Marine Corps, 1963.

INDEX

Index